GREEN AND GOLDEN TALES:
IRISH HERO TALES

GREEN AND GOLDEN TALES

IRISH HERO TALES

MICHAEL SCOTT

ILLUSTRATED BY
JOSEPH GERVIN

THE MERCIER PRESS
CORK and DUBLIN

The Mercier Press Limited.,
4 Bridge Street, Cork
24 Lower Abbey Street, Dublin 1.

First published by Sphere Books Ltd., 1985 under the title
Tales from the Land of Erin, Volume 3, A Silver Wish. This
enlarged edition, with extra stories, first published in 1989.

ISBN 0 85342 868 9

For Piers, a second addition

Printed by Litho Press Co., Midleton, Co. Cork.

Contents

The Birth of Lugh

Ireland is a land of heroes. Some of them are famous and remembered in myth and legend, some are almost forgotten.

But let us start with a tale about the birth of the first of the great Irish heroes. He was a son of one of the godlike Tuatha De Danann, and in time he became a god himself. He was also supposed to be the father of Cuchulain. He was called Lugh, and his grandfather was the terrible demon Balor . . .

Balor opened his single eye and looked out through the open window across the waves. There was a storm brewing and the sky to the east was dark with heavy clouds. The King could already see the tiny flashes of lightning on the horizon.

The demon-king looked down. He was standing in the highest room of a tall tower that was made from glass; pure crystal-clear glass — and if you looked up quickly, and didn't notice the reflections on the glass walls, you might almost think he was standing in mid-air. The island on which the tower stood was a broad, rocky, barren place off the northern coast of Erin. Nothing grew on it, no sea birds nested on its rocky cliffs, and no seals rested on its stony beaches.

They all feared the demon-king, Balor — and his Evil Eye. Balor had the power to turn anyone or anything to stone if he looked at it with his left eye, and so he always kept it covered up with a patch. He only removed the patch when he was in battle, and then he would stare and glare at his enemies, first turning them to stone and then, if he continued glaring at them, making them burst into flames.

And so, no one liked to make the terrible king angry — there was no telling what he would do. But the king was angry now.

He turned around slowly and stared hard at the tall, black-cloaked magician standing before him. 'Tell me that again,' he said in his low, rasping voice.

The magician shrugged his bony shoulders nervously. He was Moch, the Magician, one of the most feared and terrible wizards in the world — but even he was terrified of the king. He glanced across quickly at the huge fat man, with his snow-white hair and beard, his single red eye and the even more fearsome black and red eyepatch, which had the shape of an eye sewn on to it.

'Tell me!' Balor suddenly roared.

Moch coughed and looked at the thick chart he was holding in both of his hands. 'Well,' he began, 'as I said, I have looked into the future; I have read your stars; I have

used my magic mirror; I have drunk from the Waters of Memory . . .'

'Get on with it,' Balor snapped.

Moch swallowed hard. Standing on a glass floor in a glass tower with glass walls was making him feel very frightened and very sick. He kept expecting to fall straight down at any moment. He took a deep breath and hurried on. 'All of this tells me that you will be killed by the son of your daughter Eithlin.'

'My daughter is but a girl,' Balor rumbled softly, almost to himself.

'But she is such a beautiful girl,' Moch said quickly, 'and a girl of such beauty will be sure to attract many admirers. Surely one of them will seek her hand in marriage . . . ?'

Balor glared at the magician for such a long time that, even though the king wasn't looking at him with his Evil Eye, Moch still began to feel very warm. Then the demon-king nodded. 'Aye; you're right. I must make sure that she does not get to meet any young men.'

'What will you do?' the magician asked.

'Keep her here.'

'But you cannot keep her here all the time,' Moch said.

'Why not?' Balor shouted.

'But . . . but what about her schooling?' the magician asked.

'Her teachers, the bards, and scholars and the men of learning can come here to her,' the king said.

'Ah, but then she will get to meet men,' Moch said quickly.

The king nodded. 'Yes, you're right. Then she will only have women teachers and attendants.'

The magician shook his head. 'It will be very difficult to find them . . .'

'Aye,' Balor rumbled, 'and that's why you will find them for me!'

'That's impossible!'

The king frowned at the magician, and then he began rubbing his eyepatch.

'I'll do my best!' Moch said quickly.

The years passed, and Eithlin grew from a lovely girl to a beautiful young woman. However, she never left the island, and the only people she ever saw were her teachers and attendants, and the only man she ever saw was her father.

And as the years passed, Balor began to relax. He knew that there was no possible way for any man to come near his daughter.

And then the demon-king began to collect all the magical objects in the world; the swords and spears, shields and cups. He made a huge zoo and gathered all the creatures that had been made with the world, the unicorns, the dragons, the hairy elephants, the huge bird from the east, the roc, and the animals that could never die. At last there was only one magical animal that he needed, and that was a cow which gave a never-ending supply of milk.

It was owned by three brothers in Erin, men of the Tuatha De Danann.

Cian and Samthann met their brother Goibniu in his forge just as evening was falling. Goibniu was a blacksmith and the large, airy room was warm and the air tasted of hot metals and burnt coals. He was hammering a long strip of metal with hard, even strokes of his huge hammer, and his two younger brothers stood by and squinted against the hard, bright sparks which scattered along the anvil and on to the floor with every stroke.

The huge blacksmith stopped and wiped his forehead on the back of his arm. 'Another moment or two,' he panted, and then he turned back to his hammering, turning the long bar of metal into something which looked like a sword. After another five or six strokes he stopped and plunged the red-hot length of metal into a barrel of ice-cold water. There was a terrible high-pitched hissing and spluttering sound and billows of thick white steam rose up around Goibniu's head, and for a few minutes, the blacksmith's red hair and beard sparked with tiny drops of silver water.

'Now,' Goibniu said, examining the metal and then putting it down on a clean piece of cloth, 'that's done. It's a sword,' he said, seeing Cian looking closely at it. He wiped his hands on his long leather apron and then stepped away from the red glow from the fire.

'Why have you asked us to come here?' Cian asked. He was the youngest of the three brothers; a tall, thin man with dull red hair and just the beginnings of a beard on his face. He was said to be amongst the handsomest men of the Tuatha De Danann.

'Yes,' Samthann said, 'I had some planting to do, and there were cows to be milked . . .' Samthann was just two years younger than Goibniu, who was the oldest, but already he looked like an old man. His hair was almost all gone, and even his beard was growing thin. There were lines on his forehead and around his mouth.

Goibniu raised one thick-skinned hand. 'I wouldn't have asked you to come here unless it was important,' he said. He was a huge man, with thick muscles from all his years of smithying, and his red hair and bushy beard were lined with silver-grey hairs. But he was immensely strong and the most famous blacksmith amongst the Tuatha De Danann. 'I have had a message from Balor,' he said quietly.

'Balor!' Cian gasped. 'What does that demon want?'

'Well, whatever it is — he can't have it,' Samthann added.

Goibniu nodded his head, his sharp grey eyes softening as he smiled. 'That's very easy to say, but what happens if he comes after us with that Evil Eye of his?'

'We are De Danann,' Cian began, 'and we are the finest magicians in all the known world.'

Goibniu nodded again. 'What use is magic if all he has to do is just look at you? What use is magic if he turns you into a pillar of fire?' The huge man sighed, and shrugged his shoulders. 'And don't forget — he is a demon, and a powerful sorcerer himself.'

'Has he still got that magician, — what was his name? — Mach . . . Macha . . . Mocha . . . Moch . . .'

'He was called Moch,' Goibniu said softly, and then he shook his head. 'Moch was turned to stone some years ago for disobeying Balor. He now stands as a statue in the demon's garden as a reminder of what will happen to those who anger him.'

'What was the message from Balor?' Cian asked.

The blacksmith gave a little half-smile, his teeth looking very white against his darkly-tanned face. 'He wants Gabby . . . '

Cian turned pale. 'Gabby? My Gabby? He wants my Gabby? Why?' he suddenly shouted.

Goibniu put one of his large hands on his younger brother's shoulder. 'I don't know why he wants Gabby. Perhaps because she is the finest cow in the herd; perhaps because she is one of the loveliest animals in the land . . .'

'Perhaps because she gives more milk than any other animal I've ever seen,' Samthann said quietly. 'You could feed an army on what she gives alone.'

Goibniu added. 'That could be another reason. I've heard the demon is collecting magical animals.'

Cian shook his head. 'Well, he can't have her. I've raised that cow since the time she was a day-old calf. I've fed her, looked after her, taken care of her as if she were one of my own family. And I'm not going to give her to any demon.'

'If you don't, then Balor will come across from his Isle of Glass and lay waste to the land,' Goibniu said very softly. He knew how fond Cian was of the cow — they all were, she was a very special animal.

'What are we going to do?' Samthann asked his older brother.

'What can we do?' he said.

'Well, I know what we can do,' Cian said, 'not give Gabby to the demon. He'll probably eat her,' he said in horror.

'No,' Goibniu said quickly. 'He knows how valuable she is; he's not going to eat her.'

'Then *why* does he want her?' Cian demanded.

Goibniu put his arms around his brothers' shoulders and led them out of the forge. Outside, night was falling and there was the rich, wet smell of rain in the air. Already the first of the night-stars were beginning to sparkle in the sky. 'Balor is greedy,' Goibniu said at last, just when Cian was beginning to think he hadn't heard the question. 'He is the type of person who must have certain things even though they are things he will never use, or indeed, ever have any use for. People like that collect jewels, precious

metal, or indeed, anything that is rare, anything that is
scarce. And they want it because they are the only one in
the world to have it. It is theirs and no one else's.' Goibniu
paused, and then tilted his head to one side, listening.
'There is rain coming,' he said very softly, and then he
continued on with the conversation. 'He wants Gabby for
that reason — she is the only one of her kind. There is not
another cow like her in all the world. She is unique. He
wants to add her to his zoo.'

'And for no other reason?' Cian asked.

'Probably not.'

'Well, he's still not going to get her,' Cian said quickly.

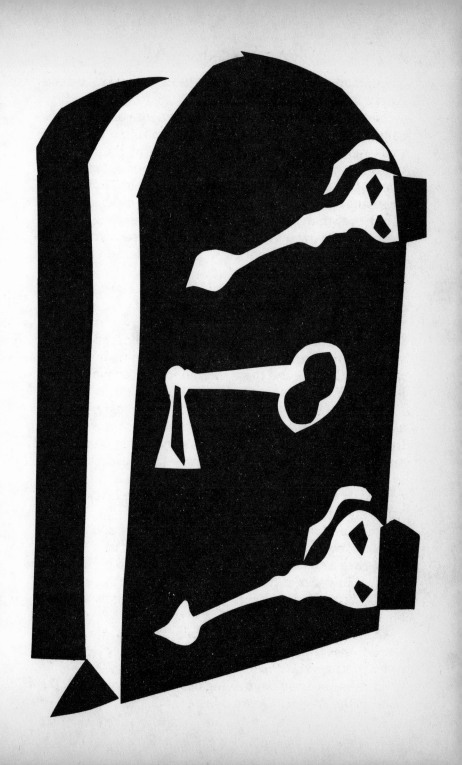

Samthann sighed. 'Well then, how long do we have before he comes to get her himself?'

'Not long,' Goibniu said. 'Here, listen for yourselves,' he said, and led his two younger brothers into a huge cave that was hidden in amongst the rocks at the foot of a mountain. There was a thick metal door fitted to the opening of the cave on hinges that were almost as big as the men. The door looked so big that they doubted that it could even move, but as they passed, it swung silently closed on its own. The two brothers tensed, expecting a terrific boom as the door closed, but it clicked shut with barely a sound.

They hurried after Goibniu down a long straight corridor and into a large round room. The cave was light and bright and there was even a fire burning in the corner with a specially made metal chimney leading up into the stone ceiling. There were also four other doors leading off this central room, and there seemed to be even more doors leading off the other rooms.

However, Goibniu crossed the room quickly, kicking aside the thick pillows that were scattered everywhere. At the far side of the room there was a wooden bird-perch, and standing on the bar was a crow — a large black, sharp-eyed crow. Goibniu reached out his hand and the bird pecked at it — its curved beak missing the blacksmith's finger by a fraction.

Goibniu glanced back at his two brothers and smiled. 'This is one of Balor's creatures — friendly, isn't it?' The crow gave a short, hoarse screech and tried to peck at him again. 'However, it does have a message for us, from the demon himself, don't you?' he asked, turning back to the bird.

The bird began to screech, but half-way through a screech the sound turned into a cackling, hoarse, almost raw sounding voice.

'... from the Lord Balor, King of the Isles, Lord of all the Land in the Western Ocean, Master of the Sea, Monarch of the Waves, Commander of the Clouds, Bringer of Storms ...'

'Enough!' Goibniu snapped, 'go on to the message.'

The crow glared at the huge blacksmith for what seemed like a very long time, and then, with an angry caw, it began. 'To the three brothers of the tribe of the Tuatha De Danann, by name, Goibniu, a smith, Samthann, a farming man and Cian, a warrior, I send you greetings.' The crow gave a quick screech then that sounded so much like a laugh that the three men jumped with fright. 'It has come to my attention that you own a magical creature. This animal — a cow — should belong to me, and I am a little surprised that you have not sent it to me already. However, I will give you three days to make up for this mistake, and if you have the animal sent to me either by boat or by magic within the next three days, I shall do nothing . . . ' The crow paused and flapped its wings. It glared at the three brothers with its sharp black eyes. 'If you do not, I will come and get the cow myself and turn you to stone. That is all.' The crow gave a final screech and fell silent.

Cian glared at the bird. 'I've a good mind to . . .' he began.

Goibniu raised a hand. 'Wait a moment — this bird will carry our reply back to Balor.' He turned back to the bird. 'You may tell your master that we will not surrender the magical cow to him. It is ours — and if he wants it, then he must come and get it.'

The crow looked at him steadily for a few moments and then it flapped its ragged wings and flew past their heads and down the corridor.

'So, what do we do now?' Cian asked when the bird had gone.

'Now we wait,' Goibniu said.

'For what?'

'For Balor,' Goibniu said with a smile.

Over the next three days, Cian took Gabby with him everywhere he went. She was a tall, almost thin animal, with huge brown eyes and a clear cream-coloured skin that felt like silk. She was one of the fairy animals which the Tuatha De Danann had taken with them on their magical metal ships when they came from the Four Cities in the north to the island that would become the Land of Erin.

As the days passed, the brothers gathered their warriors and friends, and hired mercenaries — these were wandering soldiers who would fight for pay — and surrounded their own fort with them.

The brothers sent out messages to all the lords of the De Danann, and the greatest wizards, sorcerers and magicians prepared their warlike spells and healing potions. Then they all waited the coming of Balor of the Evil Eye.

Three days passed. And nothing happened.

Balor didn't come, and the watchers on the cliffs of Erin's northern coast saw that the dark storm clouds still hung over the Isle of the Tower of Glass — as they always did when the demon lord was there.

Six days passed. Then nine, then fifteen, then twenty, then thirty . . .

Gradually, the warriors drifted away, back to their homes and farms. The mercenary soldiers were paid off, and allowed to go on their way, and the magicians and wizards put away their dusty spell books and locked up their healing herbs and potions. Perhaps Balor was too afraid to come after the animal. Perhaps he thought she wasn't worth the trouble — after all, she was only a cow. Perhaps the terrible demon wasn't as powerful as he had once been.

And so everything returned to normal — except for Goibniu, Samthann and Cian . . .

I just don't believe that he isn't coming,' Cian said, shaking his head.

'Neither do I,' Samthann added from his seat beside the door of the forge. He was sitting with his back to the wooden wall, watching the magical cow which was grazing on the rich green grassland around the forge. The cow still went wherever the brothers went.

Goibniu pounded a thin bar of metal into a smooth curve, and then laid it down on the anvil and began to hammer it again. 'Well I think he's just waiting,' he said.

'Waiting for what?' Cian said.

'Waiting for us to grow careless and take our eyes off Gabby for a moment,' the huge blacksmith said.

'Well, he's going to have a very long wait,' Cian said, and Samthann nodded. 'He will never get her.'

Goibniu smiled, his face red and warm against the firelight. 'Never is a very long time,' he said, 'and don't forget, Balor is a demon.' He swung his heavy hammer a final time, and then lifted up a glowing horseshoe. 'Now,' he said, changing the subject, 'Do you two want your swords made now?'

Cian nodded and Samthann looked back over his shoulder. 'Yes please, and we even brought our own metal.'

Cian carried a thick, cloth-wrapped bundle of metal bars over to his older brother. Goibniu examined each piece carefully and then nodded. 'It's good stuff. So,' he said looking from one to the other, 'what sort do you want?' Both men began speaking together and Goibniu raised his hands. 'One at a time please. Cian, you first, Samthann is watching Gabby. When you have given me instructions, you can go and allow Samthann to come in and tell me what he wants. Is that fair?' Both men nodded.

Now, while Cian was telling Goibniu just what sort of sword he wanted, Samthann spotted movement in the woods that surrounded the forge, and he suddenly found that all the birds had fallen silent. He stood up slowly and lifted his long throwing spear in both hands.

Something flashed in amongst the trees and he was just about to shout out to his two brothers when a small boy stepped out from the bushes. They stared at each other for a few moments and then the boy walked forward and stopped quite close to the man. Samthann saw that he was young — no more than about ten or so — with a mop of thick red hair that fell forward across his face, and bright freckles across his cheeks and nose. Samthann could only see one bright green eye peeking out from amongst the tangled curls.

The boy smiled, showing the big gaps where his front teeth were missing. 'Hello,' he said, very quietly, almost in a whisper.

Samthann nodded. 'Hello. And where did you come from?' he asked, lowering his spear.

The boy jerked his head back over his shoulder.

'Over there,' he said. 'What's your name?' he asked then.

'Samthann. What's yours?'

'Ro,' the boy said.

'Ro? That's an unusual name,' Samthann said, frowning.

'It's my nickname,' the boy said. 'My mother told me never to tell my real name to a stranger in case he was a magician and might use it in a spell over me.'

Samthann nodded. 'That's wise. But tell me, what are you doing here?'

The boy shrugged. 'Playing. I always play in these woods.' He smiled, leaned forward and then whispered, 'And sometimes I creep up to the forge and listen to the smith making shapes in metal.'

'He's my brother,' Samthann said proudly.

'Oh? Is he going to make you a sword too, then?' the boy asked.

'How did you know Goibniu was making swords?' Samthann asked curiously.

'I heard him talking to another man earlier on today,' Ro said, very quietly. 'They were talking in the wood, and one said he would bring the metal later on today, and then the big one said he would make the finest sword in all the Land of Erin. The thin man then asked if it would not use up all the metal he and his brother had bought, and the blacksmith said it would — but that there was really only enough metal for one good sword.'

Samthann frowned angrily. 'When did you hear this?' he demanded.

Ro looked a little frightened at the man's angry expression and took a step back. 'Earlier on today,' he whispered.

'They're going to cheat me!' Samthann suddenly shouted and turned around and darted into the forge.

And when he and his two puzzled brothers came out a few moments later, the small red-haired boy had gone — and so had Gabby. But right where the cow had been grazing two small bushes had been turned to stone. The boy had been Balor in disguise — and he had stolen the cow!

For many weeks afterwards, Cian went from fort to fort, asking advice from the wizards, magicians and druids, wondering how he would get his magical animal back. But they all told him that it was impossible — no one would go against the terrible Balor.

However, on the last day of summer, just when the trees were beginning to change colour and crisp dry leaves crunched beneath his horse's hooves, Cian met an old woman walking along the road. She was bent and stooped with a huge bundle of sticks on her back. Cian reined his horse in beside her and jumped down.

'Let me help you,' he said, and lifted the heavy bundle and placed it across the horse's saddle.

The old woman straightened up and pressed her hands to her back. She looked very old indeed, with a round wizened face, full of lines and wrinkles. There were strands of silver-grey hair peeking out from under the hood of her cloak. 'Thank you, young man,' she said, her voice as dry and cracked as the withered leaves. 'I live just yonder . . . if you could carry the sticks for me . . .'

'Of course,' Cian said.

They walked on in silence for a few moments, and then the old woman glanced up at Cian with her sharp black eyes. 'I don't often see warriors in this part of the country,' she said.

'I was looking for a famous druidess,' Cian said quietly, 'but no one seems to know where she is.'

'And why would you be looking for the Witch of the Mountain, eh?' the old woman cackled.

'I need to ask her advice,' Cian began, and then he stopped. 'You've heard of her?'

The old woman nodded. 'Oh yes, I know Birog of the Mountain — she is one of the few women druids in the land.'

'Do you know where she lives?' Cian asked, excitedly. 'It's important I find her.'

'Oh, she doesn't like to be disturbed,' the old woman said, shaking her head, 'and she is supposed to have a terrible temper. You never know what she might do to you if you made her angry.'

'I would still like to see her.'

'Why?'

Cian looked down at the old woman walking by his side. She looked a lot like hundreds of old country women he had seen in his travels across the land, but she had a kindly smile and her eyes were gentle. And so, as they walked along the dry dusty road, he told her about Gabby, his magical cow, and how Balor had come to steal her away.

He finished just as they came to a low building of wood and stone, that was so close to the ground and covered with grass that it was hard to tell where the earth finished and the house began. Cian lifted the bundle of sticks off his saddle and placed them on top of a pile that was stacked up before the door. He was just about to climb back up into the saddle when the old woman laid her thin, long-fingered hand on his arm.

'Would you like to go to the Isle of Glass?' she asked, very quietly, her eyes bright and shining.

'Of course,' Cian said, 'but the island is guarded and any boats that come near, Balor looks at and turns them to stone, sinking them instantly.'

'Ah, but he has to see you first,' the old woman said and then she began to laugh in a quick, high cackling voice that made the young warrior shiver. 'He has to see you,' she said.

Cian nodded doubtfully and then slowly backed away. 'Well, I must be going now . . .' he said suddenly realising that he was far from his path; the sun was already low in the sky, and the old woman might very well be a witch.

She suddenly looked at him with her bright, bright eyes and smiled. And it was as if a mask had fallen away. Years seemed to melt from her face. The lines and wrinkles faded back into her skin, which grew soft and smooth; her hair turned a dark grey and then black, and as she straightened up she seemed to grow taller. 'You have no need to fear me,' she said, and now her voice was soft and gentle. 'I am Birog of the Mountain!'

'But . . .?' Cian began, with his mouth open.

'Sometimes it is necessary to test out my callers,' Birog said, 'some of them are not all as gentle as you, nor are they as honest. Some come to steal my spells, others come to kill me.' She shrugged, and then pulled back the hood of her cloak and shook out her long black hair. 'But I am Birog of the Mountain — the most powerful sorceress in all this land.'

'Can you help me then?' Cian asked.

The witch-woman nodded. 'Of course. Now, come inside,' she added, 'night is falling and it is growing cold.'

Cian followed the druidess into the low stone building. It was very plain and simple, with thick rugs scattered over the floor and pinned to the walls. Birog crossed to the fire and poked at the smouldering ashes with a long length of metal, and then, as a thin thread of grey smoke rose up into the chimney, she scattered a pinch of grey powder on it. The fire immediately sparked and blazed with a bright blue-green flame. The druidess then quickly added some wood and turf to the blaze, and then she turned back to the warrior.

'The first thing we have to do,' she said, 'is to decide how we are going to get on to the island . . .'

'But it is guarded night and day,' Cian said, 'and neither man nor beast will get past the guards.'

'Ah, but what about a woman?' Birog asked with a strange smile.

Cian shook his head. 'I don't understand.'

'You will,' Birog promised, and she turned back to the fire.

Eithlin sat on the shore of the Isle of Glass and stared out at the shifting banks of fog that rolled over the sea. She was a small, almost fragile looking young woman, with long pale-gold hair and bright blue-green eyes, and she was so lovely that it was hard to realise that her father was Balor, the demon.

And now she was bored.

There was nothing to do on the island. She had her teachers, but there was very little left for them to teach her, and she had learned many things that perhaps she shouldn't have. She could recite the history of the world from the day it was created; she could list the kings of Erin down from the coming of the Princess Caesir Banba from the Isle of Meroe to the present day; she knew the names of the different lands that lay to the east of Erin, and of those to the north and south — and she knew that there was no land to the west.

But Eithlin could also fight with a sword, a knife, a spear, and she was a deadly shot with a bow and arrow or a sling. She also knew a little magic — but not much — because her father wouldn't allow any magician to remain on the island for long.

And even though she could do all these things, she was still bored — because there was nothing *else* to do.

Her father never allowed her to leave the island, and every night he came to her and told her terrible stories about creatures called 'men' — who looked a little like women, but were far more dangerous. Eithlin had never met a man, and so she didn't know what they looked like, but she sometimes wondered if they were anything like the creature she sometimes saw in her dreams.

Her dream was always the same. She was sitting on a beach — very much like this one — when a sudden storm blew up at sea, and huge waves washed in on to the rough stones and sand. In her dream she was walking down to the water's edge and allowing the waves to wash in over her feet. And then the waves would part and a long black bundle would be washed ashore. Eithlin would then bend down and turn this bundle over and find she was looking into a face. Eithlin didn't know what sort of face it was, except that it wasn't a woman's face — it was too broad and hard and there was some sort of sharp bristling hair growing around the chin. But it was a very nice face, a strong face, and Eithlin found she liked it. She shook the figure . . . but she always woke up just before the figure opened its eyes.

'Hello! You there — on the beach — hello!'

Eithlin jumped with fright. She had been deep in thought, wondering about her strange dream, when the voice startled her. It was coming from the sea. The young woman picked up her spear and stood, wondering what to do.

'Hello!' the voice called again. It was a woman's voice, by the sound of it, Eithlin decided.

'Who's there?' she called.

'Just an old woman and her mistress,' the voice called back, and Eithlin saw a vague shape drifting out of the fog.

'What are you doing out there?' the young woman asked.

'Our ship was attacked by pirates, and we slipped away in the curragh while the fighting was going on,' the older woman's voice called again.

The fog drifted apart and Eithlin saw a long low curragh floating in towards the shore on the tide. There seemed to be only two women in it — one was standing up and seemed to be doing all the talking, and the other was sitting in a heap by her feet. Both women were wearing long black travelling cloaks.

'Will you give us shelter until this terrible fog lifts?' the woman asked.

Eithlin thought about it for a moment. Her father had told her never to allow anyone on to this island. But she was sure he meant 'men' or creatures like that — but what harm could two women do? She nodded then and lowered her spear. 'You can rest here until the fog lifts.'

The woman who was standing raised her head and looked straight at the young woman and smiled. 'Thank you,' she said. 'Perhaps we could stay the night,' she added, 'my mistress here is very tired and needs food and rest.'

'Of course you may,' Eithlin said kindly, 'but you must be very careful not to let my father see you. He doesn't allow anyone to land on this island.'

The curragh settled on to the beach with a scraping crunch, and then tilted slightly to one side. The standing woman almost fell but Eithlin caught her, and then the second woman stood up quickly and helped the older woman down on to the beach.

'Thank you — you're both very kind,' the old woman said. 'My name is Birog, and this is . . . Ciarnat, my mistress.'

Eithlin smiled and said hello to both women, but strangely Ciarnat didn't pull back the large hood of her cloak and kept her head bent forward, so that it was impossible to see what she looked like. It was a little strange, Eithlin decided, but perhaps she was just shy. 'This way,' she said then, 'we will go back to my rooms and I'll have my servants prepare a meal for you and make up two beds. We had better hurry,' she said, 'night is falling, and my father will be home soon.'

Every evening before she went to bed, Eithlin walked along the beach. She loved to listen to the sound of the sea and hear the whispering and hissing of the water on the sand. The sound was so peaceful and restful, and she always fell asleep as soon as she climed into bed.

Eithlin crunched down the beach, her hands tucked into her long sleeves, her head bent. She was thinking. There was something about those two women who had landed earlier that evening; something wrong about them. Birog frightened her; there was something so different, so strange about her, and she reminded the young woman of her demon father.

The other woman was even stranger. Eithlin hadn't even seen her face yet. She hadn't eaten with Eithlin and Birog, and she didn't speak a word, only nodded and made little grunting sounds. Eithlin shook her head again; something about those two women was just not right.

The young woman suddenly stopped. There was someone standing on the beach ahead of her. She felt her heart begin to pound as she strained to make out the figure's shape in the darkness. As quietly and as carefully as possible, she slipped her knife free . . .

'I won't harm you,' the figure said suddenly, and then turned around and faced Eithlin.

The young woman stopped. That voice sounded so strange — so hard and strong. She had never heard anything like it before. But one thing was sure — it was not a woman's voice. She took a step forward and raised her knife. Starlight sparkled on its blade.

'I won't harm you,' the stranger said again.

'Who are you?' Eithlin demanded.

'I am Cian, a warrior of Erin,' the figure said, and pushed back the hood of a long black travelling cloak. 'I came here earlier today disguised as Ciarnat.'

Eithlin looked into the figure's face and then almost dropped her knife with shock. It was the face of the figure in her dreams. 'Are you . . . are you a man?' Eithlin asked in a whisper.

Cian nodded. 'I am a man.'

'I have never seen a man before,' the young woman said, 'my father will not allow them on this island.' She stopped and then asked, 'Tell me, what are you doing here? Why have you come?'

'I came to get something of mine,' Cian said.

'What would we have of yours?' Eithlin asked in amazement.

'My magical cow,' Cian said, and then he and Eithlin walked slowly down the beach and he told her how her father Balor had come to Erin disguised as a boy and stole Gabby, his magical cow.

Cian stayed on the island for many months; hiding by day and creeping out at night to walk along the beach with Eithlin. Eventually, they were married by Birog, and almost a year later, Eithlin gave birth to a baby boy.

Balor stamped about the palace in a towering rage. His daughter — *his daughter*, whom he had protected so carefully, and guarded, and kept from all men, had just given birth to a boy. And, what was almost as bad, he had found out that she was married to a warrior of Erin — the same one who wouldn't give up his magical animal.

If he ever got his hands on that Cian . . .

The demon-king stamped into the big airy room where Eithlin had just given birth to her son. She was sleeping now, with her servants and women standing around, gently rocking the tiny bundle asleep. They all stopped when they saw Balor.

He looked at each of them in turn, and each one shivered, expecting to be turned into a lump of stone at any moment. 'You,' he suddenly said, pointing to one, 'take the boy and come here.'

'Me, your majesty?' the woman asked timidly.

'Yes, you,' he snapped. 'Wrap up the boy and follow me.'

The woman took the boy from the arms of the nurse and, holding him very carefully, followed the demon. 'Where are we going?' she asked, when she caught up with him.

The demon glared at her from his single eye. 'A magician once told my future,' he said, 'and he foretold that I would be killed by my grandson. Well, I've done the best I could to keep Eithlin from men — but that hasn't worked. So, now I'll just have to make sure that there is no grandson to kill me.' Balor smiled then, showing his long yellow teeth, and his smile was terrible.

The woman followed the demon down along the path that led to the cliffs. He stopped at the very edge and pointed down. 'Drop the boy down there,' he commanded.

The woman crept to the edge and looked down. Far, far below, the waves pounded against the jagged rocks, sending water high into the air.

'You couldn't,' she said.

'I could,' Balor said. 'Throw him down.'

'I won't do it,' the woman said.

'Well I will,' the demon roared and went to snatch the child from the woman. She ducked away and suddenly threw herself out over the edge of the cliff — and fell down, down, down . . .

Balor began to laugh — and then he stopped. The woman hadn't struck the water. Instead, she was hovering

a few feet above the surface, with the baby boy held high in her hands.

'Look at your grandson, Balor of the Evil Eye,' she shouted, 'the next time you will see him he will be coming to kill you.' And then the woman and baby sank slowly beneath the waves.

Of course, the woman had been Birog, who had remained behind on the island to guard and protect Eithlin and the baby.

She took the baby, who would be called Lugh, and carried him away to her secret land, and there she trained him in all the arts and crafts of the land. And he became the greatest warrior in all Erin. The first of the great Irish heroes.

Balor's Pets

As Lugh grew up, Balor, his grandfather, tried to kill him many times, because he still feared Moch the Magician's prophecy that the boy would one day kill him.

However, Balor couldn't come close to Birog's land, because she had protected it with her magic. So, the demon sent some of his pets to try and kill the young boy . . .

Lugh took a deep breath and then waited while Birog slowly counted down from five.

'Five . . . four . . . three . . . two . . . one. *Go!*'

Suddenly the boy was off and running down the beach, his legs pumping up and down, his arms close by his side, punching the air, and his head down. He breathed in carefully, the way the old woman had taught him, and he kept his eyes fixed on a bright red flag at the far end of the beach.

When he reached the flag, he touched it for a single instant with his foot and then he had turned and began racing back up the beach towards Birog, his eyes now fixed on the tall, old woman. When he crossed the finishing line, he fell to the ground, gasping.

Birog bent over and ruffled his pale blonde hair. 'That was your best yet,' she said with a laugh. 'You will soon be the fastest runner in all Erin.' She glanced up into the heavens, looking towards the sun, judging the time. 'You can have a short break now, but don't go far, you have some sword practice and spear throwing to do this afternoon.'

'*Aaaw* Birog . . .' Lugh began, looking up at the old witch woman with his bright blue-green eyes, the same colour as his mother's.

'*Lugh,*' Birog said, and that one word was all the boy needed to know that if he said any more, the old woman would more than likely just double the amount of work he had to do. 'You know I am training you to be the greatest warrior Erin has ever known. You also know that I am training you to be a king, ruler of this land. And you also know that I am training you to defend yourself against your grandfather.'

'I know,' Lugh said quietly.

'Well, you should remember it,' Birog said. 'Now, go on before I change my mind about that free time.'

The boy quickly jumped to his feet and ran off down the beach. 'And don't go too far,' the old woman called after him. Lugh turned and waved before he disappeared into the sand-dunes.

The sand-dunes were huge, stretching for miles in every direction. Some were so high that it seemed impossible to climb them, and they fell down into deep sandy hollows, little hidden places cut off from the rest of the beach. The dunes were topped with long blades of sharp grass. Lugh was always careful to avoid this — it was razor-sharp and he had cut his hands and legs a few times because he had come too close to it. The grass had thin hairy roots that dug deep down into the dunes, and Birog had told him that they actually helped to hold the dunes together, stopping them from spreading inland.

Once he was into the sand-dunes, all the sounds seemed to quieten down, and even the constant pounding of the sea was softer and gentler. It was hotter too, because there was no breeze. The young boy raced up one side of a dune and down the other. He loved to feel the soft sand shift and move beneath his bare feet, and he knew that even if he fell there was little or no chance of hurting himself.

Lugh ran up the side of the tallest dune and then he stood there, just looking around. Ahead of him was the sea, bright blue and sparkling, flowing away to the very ends of the world. To his left and right lay the beach, smooth and golden, a darker colour where it had been washed by the tide and dotted with patches of green grass on the dunes. Behind him lay the land of Erin. He turned around and looked at it. It was green, a bright, rich, living green. In the distance there were mountains that seemed almost purple, topped by fleecy white clouds. He could even see birds floating on the air above the mountains.

The boy was about to look away, when a sudden thought struck him — how could he see those birds? The mountains were a great distance away. The only way he could see those birds would be if they were . . . *HUGE!*

Lugh shaded his eyes with his hands and looked up into the sky. He had very good eyesight, and as he stared at the black specks in the sky, he immediately noticed two things . . . they were indeed birds — huge birds — and they were coming towards him!

Lugh turned and ran.

He threw himself down the side of the sand-dune, curling himself up into a tight ball and rolling down in a flurry of sand. He came to his feet smoothly and then set off up the side of the next one, using his hands to dig in and pull himself up. He paused for breath and glanced over his shoulder.

The birds were much closer. There were three of them; huge, golden-winged creatures, with gleaming black talons and eyes that were much too bright and seemed far too intelligent.

The boy scrambled up over the top of the dune and again rolled down the far side into a deep hollow. As he ran for the next one, the sand began to billow and fly up in a great cloud around him, stinging his eyes, getting in his nose, mouth and ears. He looked up to find one of the huge birds was almost above his head. The creature spotted him and screamed — a long, terrifying cry that made the hair on the boy's head stand on end — and then it swooped . . .

Lugh threw himself to one side as the bird's long talons bit deep into the sand, leaving long lines on the ground. It flapped its huge wings, pulling itself upwards, and while it was circling around, another one dived at the boy. Lugh stood up and faced the creature. It was the biggest thing he had ever seen, and each of its claws were as thick as his arm. It opened its beak and Lugh saw its raw, red mouth with its long wet tongue. The bird's long claws came forward, aiming straight for the boy's chest, and it screamed just as it was about to strike . . .

The boy waited until the very last moment before throwing himself to one side, rolling to his feet and beginning to run again. However, the bird's claws struck the sand, biting deep into the soft earth. It flapped its wings, raising sand in a huge cloud around it. But was stuck fast — trapped.

Lugh raced up another dune, one of the highest, and he was just about to throw himself over the far side, when he stopped. Directly below him was a huge patch of the razor-sharp grass. If he had fallen into it he would have been cut and scratched and probably very badly hurt. He heard the flapping of giant wings behind him and looked back over his shoulder. One of the great birds was approaching, flying low over the dunes, its beak open and its eyes fixed on the boy.

And Lugh suddenly realised that he was now trapped.

Before him was the dangerous grass, and behind him was the deadly bird. What was he going to do? Suddenly he had an idea. It was dangerous — very dangerous, but if he didn't do something soon the bird was going to get him. Lugh took a very deep breath and then stood up straight.

The giant bird screamed aloud and its golden wings beat harder.

Lugh then turned his back on the bird and stretched both hands straight out in front of him — like a swimmer about to dive into the sea. He looked back over his shoulder. The bird was very close now — so close that he could smell the musty smell from its dirty feathers — and then, just as it was about to snap its beak closed on him, the boy bent his knees and launched himself off the top of the sand-dune.

The bird squawked with surprise as the boy suddenly disappeared, and then it screamed with an even greater surprise as its two dangling feet struck the top of the sand dune. Its wings lost their rhythm, and the bird collapsed in a feathery heap on to the top of the dune — and tumbled straight down into the razor sharp grass.

Lugh meanwhile had sailed out over the deadly grass and landed in a bruised bundle at the bottom of the dune, on the beach. He picked himself up and looked up at the bird which was still struggling in the grass — and then the third bird came over the top of the dune. Lugh had forgotten that there were three birds! The huge creature circled once and then flapped its wings, gathering speed, and dived down towards him.

Lugh ran then. He ran as he had never run before, pounding down the beach with all his might. He tried to remember everything the old witch had told him, but all he could hear was the flap-flapping of the wings behind him, and the bird's rasping breath. He knew it was close — very close — but exactly how close he didn't know, and he daren't look back in case he tripped and fell.

And then a shadow fell over him — a huge winged shadow. He could smell the dirty, foul odour from the bird, and he could feel its hot breath on his back . . .

It had him, he knew.

He heard a ripping, tearing sound and then something green flashed above his head. There was a snap and then a muffled boom, and he was knocked to the ground by something — but not by the bird. He lay on his back and rolled over, to find the bird had been turned into a great green ball of cold fire!

Sand crunched close to his head and then a wrinkled hand reached down and pulled him up. Birog's kindly eyes smiled down into his, and she held a long staff in her hand that was still smouldering with green fire.

'There was three of them,' Lugh began excitedly, 'and the first one . . .'

Birog raised a hand. 'I know. I was watching over you all the time. You were never in any real danger from Balor's pets. Now, while I go off and deal with the other two, why don't you do a few laps of the beach, eh? That bird very nearly caught you.'

'*Aaaw* Birog,' Lugh began.

'*Lugh!*' Birog warned, glancing sternly at him.

'All right then,' Lugh said, and set off down the beach as quickly as he could, avoiding the smouldering heap on the sands. He sighed — so much for his time off!

Balor never did manage to kill Lugh, and the boy went on to become the greatest warrior Erin had ever known. And later, in the last great battle between the Fomorians and the Tuatha De Danann, Lugh did indeed slay the evil demon.

The Blacksmith's Dog

Cuchulain is perhaps the best known of the old Irish heroes, and there are many, many tales about his short, but very adventurous, life.

But Cuchulain was not the name he was given at birth. Cuchulain was his warrior's name — and this was the name a warrior took if he wished to be remembered by some deed. Cuchulain's first name was Setanta . . .

'Setanta? Setanta?'

The boys stopped playing when they heard the shout. They all recognised the voice — it belonged to Conor, the king. They turned and looked across the flat green field to where the tall figure of the man stood beside his chariot.

One of the boys stepped forward. He was small and thin, with short black hair and sharp black eyes. His face was long and his hands and feet seemed to be a little too big for the rest of his body. He waved to his uncle. 'You called me?' he asked.

The king nodded. 'I'm going south to Chulain's Fort. He is holding a feast in my honour, and I was wondering whether you wanted to come with me?'

'Is that Chulain the Smith?' the boy asked.

'Aye,' the king nodded, 'the same.'

'I would like to go,' Setanta said slowly, looking back over his shoulder at the rest of the boys standing on the playing field, 'but . . .'

'But?' the king asked.

'Well,' Setanta said, 'can I just finish this game first?' He threw the ball he was holding high into the air and then bounced in on the flat end of his hurling stick. 'I won't be long.'

Conor smiled to himself. He could remember how, when he was a boy, he always seemed to be called away just when he was winning. 'Who is winning?' he asked.

'I am,' Setanta said, sounding surprised, as if anyone else but him could be winning.

Conor smiled again, and shook his head in wonder. Setanta was playing on his own against fifteen other boys and still winning! 'All right then,' he said, 'you can come on after me. Do you know the way?'

Setanta shook his head. 'No, but I should be able to follow the marks left by your chariot wheels.'

The king nodded a final time, and then climbed up into the wood-and-wicker chariot. He snapped the reins over the heads of the two matched horses, and they set off at an even trot down the smooth, pale road.

Setanta watched his uncle disappear in a cloud of dry dust, and then turned back to the game. He tossed the small, hard ball high into the air, and then whacked it hard just before it touched the ground. The ball whizzed out over the field.

'Let's play,' he shouted.

It was growing dark by the time Setanta finished his game, and the sun had already sunk down behind the mountains in the west. The young boy stood in the middle of the field, bouncing the small ball on the end of his hurling stick, while the rest of the boys — mostly the sons of nobles and princes — gathered up their belongings and hurried off to the fort for their evening meal.

Setanta looked up into the sky, judging just how much daylight was left. He guessed that there was an hour or so; just enough time to make his way to Chulain the Smith's fort — if he hurried.

Setanta set off down the dusty track at a run, his sharp black eyes reading the tracks left by his uncle's chariot. After a while the road disappeared into grass, and then he was following the very faintest trace — sometimes just the way the grass was bent or twisted, or if the leaves on a bush were slightly astray, or if a few had been broken as something brushed past them. Most people would have missed them, but Setanta was no ordinary boy, and he had been trained since the day he had learned to walk to be a warrior and, more importantly, to be a *great* warrior.

Setanta hurried along, following the track. He had now moved into the woods and, although night was falling and the shadows had thickened, the path was easier to follow because there was really only one track a chariot could follow through the trees. The wind came up then, a cold, biting wind blowing from the north, and the boy could smell the coming rain. Dark clouds scudded across the sky, blotting out what little light was left, and soon Setanta

found himself having to slow down to a walk, because he could see very little.

Rain began to fall then, huge heavy drops that fell through the trees, and splattered on to the leaves with quick, sharp sounds.

Setanta stopped as the first of the icy drops struck his face and head and began to slide down the back of his neck like freezing fingers. He looked up to the sky, allowing the wind and rain to touch his face and, because of his training, the boy could tell that the storm would be brief but furious. He knew then that there was no point in going on; he would only be soaked through. So, he decided to find shelter and continue on after his uncle when the rain stopped.

Chulain, the blacksmith, poured the king another drink, and then both men sat down in their high-backed chairs in front of the fire and listened to the wind howl around the fort.

'Just listen to that,' Chulain said, 'It sounds like quite a storm.'

The king nodded sleepily. He had just finished a huge meal, and had drunk a lot more than he should have done. Now he was warm and relaxed, and all he wanted to do was to go straight to bed. He had also forgotten all about Setanta.

'I wouldn't like to be out in that,' the smith continued, speaking almost to himself. He was a huge man — some people said that there was some giant blood in him — and years of working with heavy metal and an even heavier hammer had given him thick, iron-hard muscles. However, he was a great, good-humoured man, with a round red face, and eyes that were almost lost behind rolls of fat that had been wrinkled by laughing.

'Aye,' Conor said slowly, making an effort to speak clearly, 'I don't think you'll find many people out on a night like that.'

The smith nodded slowly. He was a slow, deliberate man, and he had to think about everything he did; it was probably one of the reasons he was the finest blacksmith and metal-worker in all Erin. He never rushed a job, and took his time thinking about every blow he struck with his hammer — one bad blow, or foul stroke could ruin months of work. He stood up and finished his drink in one quick swallow. 'There might be no one out tonight, but I had better let Madran out just in case.'

'Who's Madran?' the king asked, looking up from the fire, his eyes sparkling dimly in the warm light.

Chulain grinned, his smile almost cracking his face in two. 'Ach, you've never seen anything like it. He's a dog — but he's more than a dog. There's a lot of wolf blood in him, and horse too I shouldn't wonder, he's so big. I got him as a pup from an old fairy woman I mended a pot for. She said I would be remembered down through the years because of that dog.' The smith laughed. 'Well, I don't know about that; but the animal has grown up to be one of the fiercest animals I've ever seen. I let him loose at night to guard the fort and the flocks. He will tear apart anything that comes even close to the fort if one of my own men isn't with them.'

Conor nodded, his eye drooping. 'It sounds like a fine animal,' he said, and then his chin dropped on to his chest and he began to snore slightly.

The smith grinned again, and then went outside to release the chain that had been specially made to hold Madran.

It must have been close to midnight when the rain finally stopped. For a few moments Setanta didn't realise that it had stopped, because the forest was still alive with drippings and droppings and soft plinking sounds as the water fell from branches and leaves on to the soft earth.

The boy stepped out from under the shelter of the spreading branches and thick leaves of an ancient oak tree,

and looked up into the heavens. The clouds had cleared away and he could see the hard points of light that were the stars sparkling through the slowly moving branches. He shivered then — not because he was afraid, because Setanta was afraid of nothing — but because the night was very cold, and he was only wearing a short, light tunic.

Setanta blew into his hands to warm them, and then he swung his hurling stick to and fro to loosen up his stiffened neck and shoulder muscles, and began to run to warm himself up. He moved lightly, barely making a sound on the damp forest floor, and he was so quiet that he was almost on top of some of the night animals before they saw him.

And faint, very faint in the distance, he heard the chilling howl of a wolf.

The trees ended suddenly and then Setanta found himself standing at the bottom of a low hill. There was a fort on the crown of the hill. The boy stopped and looked around — this must be the place he was looking for. The area around the fort had been cleared and he could see the dark patches in the earth where trees had been dug up, so no enemy could hide behind them. Setanta looked up the hill towards the fort. He could see the warm glow of light burning through the chinks in the tall fence that surrounded the fort — but strangely, there seemed to be no guards.

He stopped; that was wrong. There should be guards.

Setanta stood still at the base of the low hill while he slowly counted up to one hundred. But in that time, he still saw no guards, nor was there any sign of hidden men. But then, what was protecting the fort from attack? There had to be something — hadn't there?

But if there was, he couldn't see it.

Setanta gripped his hurling stick in both hands. He was carrying no weapons, other than the stick and the ball, and he wasn't sure what good they would do him if he were attacked. With a deep breath, he began to walk slowly up the hill towards the fort.

Meanwhile, in the fort, before the huge roaring fire, Conor, the king, mumbled in his sleep, and tossed in a troubled nightmare in which he had forgotten something very important . . .

Setanta was half way up to the fort when he stopped, his heart beginning to pound. Had he just heard something? Standing quite still, he slowly turned his head, opening his eyes wide to catch as much light as possible. But nothing seemed to be moving. He waited until his heartbeat had slowly settled down again, and then he took another step and then another . . .

There!
He had heard something! Something moving through
the short grass ... something was coming towards him ...

In the fort a log dropped in the fire, and the sudden
popping sound made the king awaken. For a moment he
didn't know where he was, and the images of his
nightmare danced before his eyes and were confused with
the glowing embers and half-burned logs in the huge
fireplace. There was something he had forgotten.
Something important. Something he had meant to tell the
blacksmith, and then there was something the smith had
told him, something which was connected to it. He shook
his head and pressed his hands to his eyes. What was it?
What was it?

Grass rustled again, and then it was as if a shadow had
taken life and rose up on four legs. There was a dog facing
Setanta. A huge animal, almost as tall as he was, with a
coat of fine, coal-black hair, glowing red eyes, and long,
yellow-white teeth. The wolf-dog growled deep in his
throat and then it began to pad towards the boy, moving
faster and faster and faster, until it was bounding towards
him, its mouth open wide ...
    The animal howled savagely, and the terrifying sound
ripped through the night.

Then Conor, the king suddenly remembered! Setanta was
coming. The boy was supposed to follow him on to the
blacksmith's fort. But the king hadn't told Chulain and he
had released his huge wolfhound guard-dog.
    The king ran to the door, and flung it open. 'Chulain ...
Chulain,' he shouted. He ran down the dining chamber,
calling for the smith, and his shouts quickly brought the
fort awake.
    The blacksmith appeared, red-faced and panting.
'What's the matter?' he gasped.

'Setanta is coming,' Conor quickly explained, 'he was to follow me here, but I forgot.'

'Madran!' Chulain said, all the colour draining from his face 'It'll tear him to pieces.'

Outside, the wolfdog howled again.

Setanta watched the animal bounding across the grass towards him. He couldn't run. There was nowhere to go, and besides, the dog would quickly bring him down.

The animal howled, and howled again, its jaws seeming to open even wider as it neared the defenceless boy. It was going to feed . . .

And then Setanta tossed the hurling ball into the air and drew back his arm and, with the hurling stick held tightly in both hands, he struck the ball a terrific blow as it fell. It took off like a stone fired from a slingshot — straight down the animal's open mouth!

The wolfhound was dead before it hit the ground.

A long shaft of light darted out from the fort as the doors were flung open and then the huge shadow of the smith stood in the open door.

'Madran, Madran,' he called, although his voice was shaking.

A small dark-haired boy loomed up out of the shadows and faced the blacksmith. 'I'm afraid I've killed your guard-dog,' he said.

'Oh,' was all Chulain could say.

'I can't pay for him,' the boy continued quickly, 'because I've no money. But what I will do is to come and guard your fort every night for the next three years. Will that repay you for the cost of the dog?'

Chulain could only nod.

'Then I will be your guard-dog,' Setanta said quietly.

And so Setanta took the place of Chulain the Smith's guard-dog. He soon got a nick-name, and that name was Cuchulain, which is the Irish for 'Chulain's dog'.

The Salmon of Knowledge

Finn MacCumhal commanded the Knights of the Fianna which guarded and protected Erin's shores from the fierce invaders from across the seas, and they kept the roads safe and free from bandits and outlaws.

Finn was one of the wisest of the old Irish warriors; a tall proud man, kind and courteous and his bravery was legendary even in his own lifetime. However, he had the strange habit of sucking his thumb when he was deep in thought. No one ever had the courage to ask him why, until one day his son Oisin managed to get some sort of answer from him, and that answer was strange enough, because all Finn would say was, 'the Salmon of Knowledge . . .'

The Salmon of Knowledge was no ordinary fish. It was the length of a tall man and about as broad, and its scales were the colours of oil on water. It was the oldest fish in all Erin — indeed, in all the world — and the wisest. Some people said that it was not really a fish, but one of the *Sidhe* folk, enchanted into the form of a huge salmon. Others said that it was the first creature that had come into this world, and still others said that it was a water-demon disguised as a fish.

But the Salmon of Knowledge was none of these; it really was a fish — but an ancient magical creature. It had once been an ordinary salmon, but that had been hundreds of years ago, when the Tuatha De Danann had first come to the land of Erin. About that time, the fairy folk had decided to hide all their knowledge and learning in seven hazel trees, to protect it from the demon Fomors. These enchanted trees had been protected by a magical well which held a demon. However, shortly after the Seven Trees of Knowledge had been planted, a young girl called Sinann had crept into the hidden forest and attempted to pick the hazelnuts which held all the secrets and lore of the De Danann folk. And then the demon had erupted from its well, catching the girl in its watery paws and throwing her high into the air, before it tore through the countryside, cutting a wide and deep path across fields and through forests until it eventually reached the broad Western Ocean in the west and south of Erin.

And people called the mighty river the Sinann, in memory of the girl who had paid a terrible price for her greed. As time passed, and the country people said the name in different ways, it changed from Sinann to Shannon, and so it remains.

However, just as people forgot about Sinann, so too did they forget about the Seven Trees of Knowledge which stood around the magical well which fed the river. As the seasons passed, the hazelnuts on the trees swelled and grew, and eventually they fell off, into the river. A salmon, an ordinary, long, fat salmon, came along . . . and swallowed the nuts.

And immediately, it knew all the ancient magic and hidden lore of the Tuatha De Danann. It became the wisest creature in the world. It became the Salmon of Knowledge.

The legends slowly grew up around the fish, and soon people began to try and catch it, thinking that if they ate the fish they would know everything it did.

But because the salmon knew everything, it knew that people would be after it, and it always managed to avoid their traps.

And then Finn came along.

He was still a young boy then, black-haired, black-eyed, tall and thin, not more than ten years old at this time. He was travelling around Erin, learning the different arts and crafts that a young prince had to know in those days. He was trained in the history and geography of Erin and the lands that lay off her shores; he learned how to run and jump, how to use a sword and spear, a bow and arrow. He also learned how to play *fidchell*, an old Irish board game, like chess.

Amongst the other arts a young warrior-prince had to learn was that of poetry. Irish folklore and legends were not written down then, but were passed on in the form of long poems and sagas, and princes were expected to know the legends of their own land. So, Finn went looking for Finegas, a famous hermit-poet who lived by the banks of the river Boyne and was supposed to know every legend and tale in the land.

He searched up and down the river, but it wasn't until late in the year, just as the trees were beginning to shed their leaves, that he finally discovered him.

Finn parted the leaves of the bush carefully and looked out across the river, towards a small, man-made hut of branches and bushes tied together. There seemed to be no one about, although the fire in front of the hut was still smouldering, and a pan of water had been put on to boil — so long ago now that most of it had turned to steam.

The boy gently eased the branch back into place, making sure no leaf quivered, remembering his training. Look first, then wait, then look again. It was a guide used by hunters when they were chasing the wild boar or deer. Of course, it could also be used for hunting another human. Finn wasn't hunting the famous poet — he just wanted to make sure that it really was the old man, and secondly to make sure that there was no one with him. These were dangerous times, and there were many people looking for the young boy, Finn.

Suddenly a bird stopped singing above his head. The boy froze. He seemed to fade into the bush, and his short tunic of green and his deeply-tanned brown skin blended in perfectly with the branches and leaves. Someone was coming. He parted two leaves and peered out again at the little camp-site.

For a few moments everything was as it had been and then an old man stepped into the clearing. He was quite small, very thin, and was wearing a long robe that had once been white, but which was now grey, and had been shortened at the end by roughly tearing off a long strip. His face was long and thin, and there were deep wrinkles on his forehead and down along the side of his nose, as if he frowned a lot, but his eyes were a bright, brilliant blue. He was humming contentedly to himself as he sat down on the river bank and lifted a simple fishing rod from the ground. The rod was no more than an old branch with a length of string attached.

When he had been fishing for a few moments, he suddenly looked up from the still, blue water — straight towards Finn's hiding place. 'You can come out from there,' he said quietly, his voice surprisingly rich and strong for such an old man. 'I know you're in there.'

Finn held his breath, but said nothing.

'I know you're there,' the old man said again. He paused, and then added, 'I am only a poor poet; all I have is what you see. I have no money, no clothes, and no possessions — so I've nothing for you to steal.'

'I'm not a thief!' the boy said indignantly, and stepped out from the bush. And then, suddenly realising that the old man had tricked him into revealing himself, he smiled sheepishly.

The old man looked over at the dark-haired, dark-eyed boy and laughed. 'You see,' he said, 'there is a power in words. Words can heal and hurt people — they can also make them angry enough to show themselves,' he said with a smile.

Finn smiled back. 'I'm sorry I was hiding — but you can't be too careful these days. I came here to look for Finegas, the hermit-poet, but I wanted to make sure that he hadn't any guests first, or even worse, that I might have stumbled on the wrong camp altogether. I've been looking for you for a long time now.' He paused, and then asked, 'You are Finegas?'

The old man bowed slightly. 'I am Finegas.'

Finn nodded. 'I thought so.' He stopped, and then said, 'Tell me, how did you know I was here?'

Finegas shrugged his bony shoulders. 'Every bush is quivering slightly in the breeze this afternoon — every bush that is, except the one in which you were hiding. I assume you were holding on to the branches?'

Finn nodded.

'It wasn't moving with the breeze, and therefore someone must have been holding it,' Finegas finished.

'Are you never afraid living here on your own?' the boy asked.

The hermit-poet shook his head. 'As I've said, I have nothing worth stealing, and most people are a little afraid of me, and so they leave me alone. Also, I know a little magic — every poet does — and so I can always frighten them away. And now,' he said, fixing Finn with his bright blue eyes, 'I've answered all your questions, would you like to answer one or two of mine?'

Finn bowed. 'I am very sorry; I was forgetting my manners. My name is . . . Demman, and I have come here to ask you to teach me some of your lore and poetry. I have been told that no one knows more than you.' The boy didn't want to give his name, in case the poet told anyone else. At that time Finn MacCumhal was being hunted by many people who wished to kill him.

'Well, that's two of my questions,' Finegas said, 'and I suppose it will do for the moment.'

'Does that mean you'll accept me as a student?' Finn asked excitedly.

'I didn't say that,' the old man said. He stared into the waters of the small, still stream and then a smile crept up across his face. 'You know, I've never had a student before . . . it might be enjoyable teaching you a little of what I know.' He looked over at the boy. 'You'd better have a good memory,' he warned.

'Oh, I have, I have,' Finn promised.

'Well, I'll soon make it even better,' the old man said. 'Now, come around here, and we'll start right away.' He pointed off down the riverbank to where the humped back of a stone could be seen in the middle of the river. 'There's a bridge of stepping-stones down yonder; you can come across there.'

Finn laughed. 'But I've just finished learning how to run and jump properly,' he said and, with both legs tightly together, he bent his knees, and jumped straight across the river, landing with a thump beside the old poet.

'Well, at least that proves you are what you say you are,' he said, 'if you had been telling me a lie, you would have walked down to the stones, instead of jumping across like any other young man learning to be a warrior. Here, sit beside me and take this.' He pushed the fishing pole into Finn's hands as soon as he had sat down on the damp grass. The poet then lay back flat on the earth and closed his eyes.

Finn had opened his mouth to say something when the old man spoke, 'We might as well start now,' he said, and then he immediately launched into an ancient poem:

> 'From the land to the east
> came the woman
> with her slaves
> and her ships
> fleeing the destruction
> of her island.'

Finegas suddenly stopped. 'Now say that back to me,' he said.

Finn coughed. 'Ahem; from ... from the land ... the land to the west, no, the east, a woman came with her slaves ...'

'*Stop!*'

The boy looked over his shoulder, but the old poet was still lying back on the earth with his eyes closed. 'I'm sorry,' he began, 'but there's no rhyme to it ...'

'Not all poetry rhymes,' Finegas said wearily. 'Now, listen to me; this poem tells about the coming of the princess Caesir Banba to Erin with her warrior-women when this island was tiny. She lived on a small island called Meroe in the great river Nile but when a great flood threatened to destroy the island she left and sailed west — to here. Her sorceress made this island grow, and later the Partholonian people did the same when they arrived, as did the Tuatha De Danann when they landed. Banba as you know, was one of the earliest names for Erin, and it was called after the Egyptian princess. Now, I'll start again, "*From the land to the east ...*"'

So, Finn stayed with the old poet and he spent many hours every day sitting by his side, reciting the ancient sagas and tales, repeating them after Finegas. The poet spent most of the day fishing and even when he retired to his tiny wooden hut beneath the trees for the night, he usually left some fishing lines drifting on the water.

But, what Finn found very strange was that Finegas didn't like fish, and always threw back any that he caught. Finn often asked him what he hoped to catch, if not a fish, but the old man would only smile, and shake his head.

Now, one day, shortly after the year had turned towards summer, and all the forest flowers began to burst into bloom, and the air was rich and thick with the smell of growing things, Finn, who had been gathering firewood, suddenly heard Finegas shout aloud. The boy grabbed his short spear and came running, thinking that some wild animal had attacked the old man. He moved swiftly and silently through the forest, heading towards the river, but when he burst through some bushes on to the bank with his spear levelled, he found Finegas lying back on the ground struggling to hold a huge wriggling salmon!

'Quick . . . quick,' the old man gasped. 'I don't think I can hold him much longer.'

Finn lifted his spear to stab the fish, but the old man shouted, 'No. You mustn't spill any of his blood. Just hold him.'

The boy dropped his spear and grabbed the huge fish by the tail. His hands slipped and slid on the slippery scales, and the fish managed to slip its tail from his hand and then it cracked him across the head, back and forth, quicker than the eye could see. Finn staggered back, seeing bright spots of colour before his eyes, his ears stinging and there were bells ringing in his head. But he was angry now.

The huge salmon slipped from Finegas' hands and began to wriggle towards the water. Finn grabbed it around the middle this time and lifted it high over his head in both hands. It was incredibly heavy — far heavier than it should be. The muscles in his neck and arms bulged and he gritted his teeth with the effort. But he held it up in the air until it had stopped wriggling and its dangerous tail hung limp.

Finegas climbed slowly and painfully to his feet. He peered up at the fish and then prodded it with one bony finger. 'Is it dead?' he whispered.

'I hope so,' Finn gasped, 'I can't hold it much longer.' He then took a step forward and threw it down on to a thick bed of moss. He almost expected it to begin wriggling again, but it didn't move. He eased his aching shoulders and then rubbed his face where the fish had hit him. One of his ears was already beginning to swell up, and there were the beginnings of a bruise around his eye. 'What sort of a fish is that?' he asked the poet curiously. 'It can't be normal.'

A strange, greedy gleam had come into Finegas' eye. 'It's a . . . an old species of salmon,' he said cautiously. 'This must be one of the last ones left alive.'

'What do we do with it?' the boy asked.

'Eat it,' Finegas said.

'But you don't like fish,' Finn reminded him.

'Ah, yes, well this . . . this old species of fish is supposed to make beautiful eating. I think I might try some of it.' He nodded. 'Now, you clean it and then cook it on the spit, and you can call me when it's ready.' He was about to turn away, when he paused and looked sternly at Finn. 'But whatever you do, do not touch a morsel from this fish before I eat it — is that understood? I've waited a long time to catch this fish, and I think I deserve first bite.'

'I won't touch it,' Finn promised.

'See that you don't' Finegas warned. 'I'm going off to rub some ointment on my bruises, and then I'll rest for a while.'

'I'll call you when it's done,' Finn promised.

The boy then set about cleaning out the fish and making it ready to cook. He then started a fire in the small patch of earth that was surrounded by stones where they did all their cooking. When the fire was burning well, with no smoke, because smoke would ruin the flavour of the fish, he set up the spit. It was made from two Y-shaped sticks which were set into the ground at either end of the fire. Another long stick rested across these, and this was put through the salmon, so that the fish was now suspended just above the flames.

Finn sat cross-legged before the fire, staring at the fish, wondering what was so special about it, wondering why the old man was so insistent that he be the first to eat it. The salmon was certainly bigger than any he had ever seen before, and it was definitely heavier than any he had ever held before. But other than that it looked like a normal salmon; well, perhaps its flesh was brighter and its eyes sharper, but he could have been imagining that.

The underside of the salmon was now cooked and he slowly turned the spit. Fat and grease spat and sizzled in the fire, and tiny sparks rose up in lazy circles.

'Is that fish cooked yet?' Finegas suddenly called from his hut.

'Not yet, another few minutes,' Finn shouted back. He leaned forward to turn the fish again. Grease suddenly spat and splashed on to his thumb. Finn wrinkled his face in pain and then popped his burning thumb into his mouth . . .

And he suddenly knew.

He knew the entire history of the Land of Erin; he could name the tribes that had conquered the land, their leaders, where they had come from. He suddenly knew the names of every plant and flower, bird, beast and insect in the forest. He could tell the names of the stars and how they had come to be called that. He knew. *He knew everything.*

He had just tasted the Salmon of Knowledge.

Of course, Finegas was not too pleased with the boy, but there was nothing he could do. Finn had been the first to taste the fish , and now he knew everything — even magic. Suddenly the boy was the most powerful man in all Erin.

And after that, whenever Finn was troubled or whenever he wondered about something, he would stick his thumb into his mouth and call up the magic of the Salmon of Knowledge, and he would suddenly know.

The Running Man

When Finn became chief of the Fianna, he gathered together the finest warriors in all the land of Erin. And while they were all warriors, they each had a special talent; some were magicians, others were strong, some were clever, or great storytellers and bards or swift runners.

They kept Erin safe from thieves and pirates, and guarded the roads from bandits. They killed the dragons that lived in the lakes, and hunted down the wild boars that killed the farm animals. They also did battle with the Fir Mhor that lived in the secret places of the land — the Giants . . .

Conn, the shepherd-boy, leaned on his long stick and looked down the mountainside over his huge flock of sheep. From where he was standing they looked like small balls of wool rolling about on green cloth. The young man sighed and pushed his long hair out of his eyes; being a shepherd could be a very lonely job, and there were times when whole weeks went by before he saw anyone or spoke to another human. Most times, Conn didn't mind; he was a quiet boy, with few friends, and he preferred his own company. Conn was also a dreamer, and watching the sheep gave him time to himself to think and to dream. And Conn's greatest wish and dream was to become one of the Fianna, the special band of warriors that Finn MacCumhal had banded together to guard Erin from its enemies.

But he knew that there was little chance of a simple shepherd and the son of a minor chieftain becoming one of the Knights.

The boy was about to turn back up the hill to the small cave where he usually spent most of the day in the shade, when he saw something moving far down in the field. He shaded his dark eyes with his hands and stared down across the fields to the line of trees and bushes that lined the rough track. But he could see nothing — only the trees quivering slightly in the breeze.

And then Conn suddenly realised that there was no breeze that day.

The boy dropped to the ground and began to creep as quickly as possible down the hill, moving from rock to rock, hiding behind the stones, but never taking his eyes from the trembling trees. There was something down there, he was sure of that now. It could be a wild animal, an elk, a boar, a wolf, or wild horse, and then again, it might be thieves trying to steal one of his father's fat sheep. Conn pulled his sling from his belt and slipped one of the round pebbles he carried in the pouch on his belt into the leather loop. Well, whoever or whatever they were, he would make sure they got nothing!

The trees shook again and this time all the sheep began to bleat and cry out, and they all trotted quickly to the other side of the field, away from the trees.

And then a hand parted the branches and an eye stared out at the animals.

It was a big hand. A huge hand with dirty fingernails the size of a warrior's shield. It was the hand of a giant.

The huge eye closed and then Conn saw another, and another, and another, and another . . . The boy closed his own eyes and squeezed them shut, thinking he must be seeing double. But when he opened them again, the creature with all the eyes was still there. It was indeed a giant — a five-headed giant!

The giant ripped the tree up out from the soil, and began

pulling off the branches, stripping it down to a long, bare log. Having five heads, and ten eyes, but only two pairs of hands, made this a difficult job, and the five heads also kept arguing with each other. When the giant was satisfied, he tested it out by smashing a rock not far from the hiding boy to dust, and then he set off after the sheep. He raised his huge stick high and then stopped . . .

Something had just hit him on the back of the neck — his third neck, that is. Head number three swivelled around, while the rest of him kept looking straight on. In the confusion he tripped and fell over his own legs. All his heads began arguing.

'Whose fault was that?'

'Not mine; I was looking where I was going.'

'It's his fault.'

'No, it's not, it's his; he turned around.'

The heads turned on their long necks and faced in to the middle one. This was Damh, the biggest head of all, and certainly the ugliest, with big ears and a flat nose. 'I turned around because something hit me,' he growled.

'What hit you?' the first head, called Dibh, asked with a sneer. He didn't like the third head, and thought that he should be the chief head.

'Maybe a bee stung you,' the second, Dubh, said. He was a friend of Dibh's, and didn't like Damh.

'Hold on a moment,' Dobh, the left-hand head, said. 'There's something over there.'

'Where?' Domh, *his* friend, asked.

'There,' Dobh said, taking over one of the two pairs of hands to point over to a clump of stones.

Dibh, Dubh, Domh and Damh turned and looked in the direction Dobh was pointing. Ten eyes — five different colours — glared at the tiny figure of the boy as he loaded another stone into his slingshot. They saw him whirling it around his head and then they saw his arm straighten.

Something buzzed through the air, and Dibh gave a shout. 'That was a stone. He hit me!'

'Right,' Damh, the biggest head said, 'we'll grab a few sheep for lunch and then we'll go after him.'

'We'll crush him,' Dibh said.

'Turn him into soup,' Dubh said.

'Into jelly,' Dobh added.

'Into mush,' Domh said.

Damh, the big head, sighed. He was a vegetarian; he ate only grass and leaves, and the few fields of vegetables he could find lying around. He didn't like shepherd pie.

The five-headed giant stooped down and scooped up a few handfuls of sheep and stuffed them into different pockets. Two of the heads kept watch, two more gathered the sheep, while the fifth watched the boy. It saw him pick up another stone — a big one this time — and fit it into his sling. It saw him twirl and sling around and around until it was nothing but a blur, and then it saw the boy's arm straighten. The head ducked.

The rock buzzed through the air and struck the giant fairly in the chest with a solid thud. Five mouths went *'oh'* — and then all the heads turned in the direction of the boy. Conn gave a quick yelp of fright when he saw the terrible expressions on their faces and turned and ran, weaving and dodging through the rocks and stones, heading into the forest.

'After him,' Dibh shouted.

'Catch him,' Dubh said.

'Don't let him get away,' Dobh roared.

'There he goes,' Domh pointed down into the trees.

'We'll never catch him now,' Damh said glumly. 'Let's go home.'

The five heads looked after the fleeing boy and saw him disappear into the forest. If they were to follow him in, it would mean uprooting all the trees to catch him, or else crawling on hands and knees — and with five heads, that could be very difficult.

One-by-one they nodded. 'Let's go home.'

At first no one would believe Conn when he told his story in his father's fort later that evening. He was terribly frightened and it took a long time for his parents to make any sense out of what he was saying. But eventually, when they finally managed to piece his story together, and heard the story of the five-headed giant, they didn't really believe him. Conn had told stories about wolves before which had turned out to be lies.

But the boy had been so frightened that Conal and Cethlenn, his father and mother, then asked the advice of an ancient druid, wondering whether their son was indeed telling the truth.

The old man had stared deep into a cup of clear water and then slowly nodded his head. 'I see the monster with heads of five. It has come.'

'But what should we do?' Conal asked the druid.

'You must send for the Fianna,' the old man said softly, and then he would say no more.

And so, later on that night, just as the moon was beginning to rise over the mountains, a black-winged hawk flew from Conal's fort and headed away towards the north and east. It was a messenger bird, asking help from Finn and the Fianna.

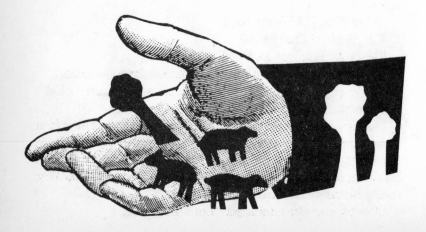

Five days later, a small, thin man came to the Fort and asked to see Conal. But the chief of the fort was out in the fields checking his cattle and sheep with his herdsmen, counting each animal, trying to work out just how many the giant had stolen so far. The small man trotted over to the chief, moving easily across the soft, boggy ground.

Conal and his herdsmen looked up as the stranger approached. 'Who are you?' Conal demanded, as soon as the man came close, 'and what are you doing on my land?'

'One of the guards told me I would find you here,' the thin man said. 'I am Caoilte, a Knight of the Fianna.'

Conal's face widened in a broad smile. 'Then you have come. You are going to slay this terrible creature for me?' And then he looked beyond the single man. 'But where are the rest of you?'

Caoilte smiled shyly. 'There is only me,' he said softly. He was a small, young man — indeed, he couldn't have been more than eighteen summers, but already his hair and eyebrows were silver-grey, the same colour as his eyes. He was wearing the simple, short robe of the Fianna, with a broad leather belt around the middle. He wore a short sword strapped across his back and carried a long hunting spear in his left hand.

'Just you?' Conal asked in amazement. 'Just *you!*'

Caoilte nodded. 'Just me, I'm afraid.'

The chieftain began to grow angry. 'I sent to the Fianna asking for help — and when I asked for help, I meant something like an army. There is a giant, a five-headed monster, destroying my crops and killing my animals — and Finn sends me a single man. Is this a joke?' he suddenly shouted.

Caoilte shrugged and smiled. 'But it's only one giant,' he said in astonishment. 'Even I should be able to manage one giant.'

'A five-headed giant?' the chieftain asked.

Caoilte nodded. 'Even a five-headed giant.'

'He will kill you,' Conal warned, 'kill you and eat you. My son said that the giant wanted to eat him.'

'I don't think this creature will kill me,' the Knight said. 'Your son has seen this creature then?' he asked.

Conal nodded. 'Aye, he was the first to see the monster — and it very nearly killed him.'

'Well then, I'll want your son to take me to the spot where he first saw the giant . . .' Caoilte began.

'You're serious,' Conal said suddenly, 'You're actually going to go in search of this giant on your own.'

Caoilte nodded.

'Well then you are either very brave, or else very mad,' the chieftain nodded, turning away. 'Stay here, I'll send my son to you.'

The Knight stood patiently in the muddy field watching the chieftain and his servants hurrying away, glancing over their shoulders at him, obviously thinking that he was mad. He smiled to himself. He didn't see what all the fuss was about — after all, it was only one giant, even though it had five heads. He gave a little laugh. He *really* didn't see what all the fuss was about.

A little while later Conn came running out across the field, very excited at finally meeting one of the Knights of the Fianna. He stopped in front of the small, rather plain man, and he looked so disappointed that Caoilte had to laugh.

'What's wrong?' he asked.

The boy shrugged and shook his head. 'Nothing . . . it's just . . . it's just I expected . . .'

'Someone different?' the Knight asked.

Conn nodded.

'Perhaps you were expecting a tall, proud warrior in gleaming bronze armour and leathers, a huge sword by his side and a tall spear in his hand. Perhaps you were even expecting a chariot?'

Conn nodded again. 'Something like that,' he confessed.

Caoilte laughed. 'But not all the Fianna look like heroes. Finn does, and so does Goll; they truly look like heroes. The rest look. . . they look just like ordinary men. Some are fat, others thin, some are bald. The sort of men you might find in your father's fort. Ordinary men.' He shrugged. 'A lot like me.'

'But you are all special; you can all do special things,' the boy insisted.

'Everyone can do special things,' Caoilte said, 'it's only a matter of finding out what your own special gift is, and then training that gift.'

'And what's your gift?' Conn asked.

'I run,' Caoilte said.

Conn didn't look very impressed. 'Come on,' he said at last, 'I'll take you to where I first saw the creature.'

'Tell me about it,' Caoilte said.

As they hurried across the fields and through the woods, heading for the mountains, Conn told the Knight about the five-headed giant. Most of the time Caoilte listened in silence, but sometimes he asked the boy a question about the creature, wondering what it had done, how it had moved and what it had said — and so, by the time, they reached the mountainside, Caoilte had a very good idea just what the monster was, and more importantly, just how he could defeat it.

The giant was sleeping, Dubh's head lying on Dibh and Dobh's lying on Domh. Damh's head was slumped down on its long winding neck on to his chest. The five heads were snoring slightly, and each one was making a different sound, a snort, a gasp, a buzz, a sniffle and a grunt. From the distance it sounded like a herd of pigs rooting in the mud, or a gaggle of geese squabbling together.

Damh raised his huge head sharply. He had heard something. He looked down over the mountainside, but there seemed to be no movement. Perhaps it was just the breeze whistling through the long grass.

There was a sudden flash of movement, and then a small human appeared, standing down by a large boulder on the hill. The figure moved and disappeared behind the stone — and then reappeared, only nearer this time.

Damh roared, bringing his other heads awake.

'What?'

'What's wrong?'

'What?'

'What's happened?'

'*There!*' Damh shouted, pointing towards the man — but there was no one there. He looked around in amazement; where had the man gone?

'Is this your idea of a joke?' Dibh asked sharply.

'Well, I don't think it's very funny,' Dubh, his friend, said.

'There was someone down there,' Damh insisted angrily. He was getting very tired of Dibh and Dubh, and if they weren't his own heads, he would certainly have knocked them together.

'Who — or what — was down there?' Dobh asked patiently.

'And where has it gone?' Domh asked.

'There was a man,' Damh said, 'a small human.'

'He must be very stupid to spy on us . . .' Dibh began and then he too stopped. He had seen something moving. 'There is something down there,' he said softly.

'Perhaps the humans are laying a trap for us,' Dubh suggested.

'Perhaps,' Dibh said. He swivelled around on his long neck and looked in at Damh. 'Well, you're the big head, what should we do?'

Damh looked uncomfortable for a few moments. He was really a quiet gentle person who disliked fights and trouble, and would much rather have preferred living quietly by himself. He sighed. 'We'd better go down and see where — *there! Ouch!*' He suddenly shouted as a small human darted right in front of the giants and jabbed them in the big toe with his spear. Five mouths opened and ten eyes squeezed shut in pain. There was another jab, and

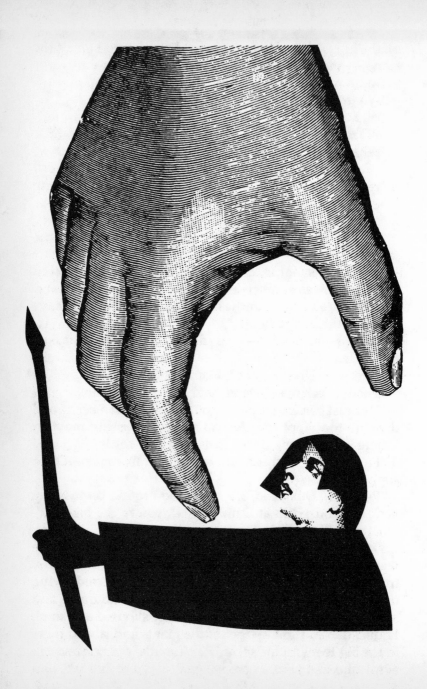

then another, and then another as the small human seemed to be everywhere at once, darting in faster than any human possibly could, stabbing with his spear, jabbing their toes, their ankles, their shins.

Damh managed to gain control of the hands for a few moments and made a quick grab for the running man. He missed by a fraction and stubbed his little finger on a rock. The rock toppled over on to the giant's finger. 'Get him,' he screamed.

Suddenly the man was running straight for them. Ten eyes opened wide, wondering what the tiny creature was attempting to do — and then the man ran straight in between their legs. Five heads bumped together as they bent to follow him, and then the body fell over as they attempted to turn as quickly as possible to follow the man.

Huge hands pounded the dirt, making the ground quiver and tremble, but the man continued running, darting, twisting, turning, slipping in and stabbing at the giant with his spear. Damh took control of the hands and began to pull up boulders from the ground. Each of them was bigger than the tiny running man. He then allowed Domh to have control; he was the best stone thrower.

Domh waited until the man was just about to begin running in again, then he threw. The stone ploughed into the ground right where the running man had been standing but a few moments earlier. Again and again, Domh threw the stones, and again and again, they missed, and always only by a fraction.

The five heads began to fight then. Each one wanted to take over the body and stop the running man. It was like a huge elephant being annoyed by a fly.

'Let me.'

'No, let me.'

'It's my turn.'

'No, it's mine.'

'I'll stop him.'

And then Damh shouted above the noise. 'There he is, after him.' The giant was pointing towards the small figure of the man as he ran across the field towards a long line of bushes. And, he seemed to be running a little slower. 'We have him now,' Damh shouted, 'he's tired out.'

The giant lumbered after the man. Although he was not usually a fast runner he was now moving downhill, and he soon began to pick up speed. Soon the giant was half-running and half-sliding — but he was also catching up on the man.

The man stopped before a line of bushes and faced the creature. He bent over, gasping for breath.

'We have him now,' Dibh, Dubh, Damh, Dobh and Domh roared together and pounded on right up to the man.

Just as the giant reached him, the man straightened up and darted right through the giant's moving legs. The giant tried to stop, but he was moving too fast — much too fast. The five-headed creature crashed through the bushes — and sailed out over the edge of a cliff!

And the last sounds Caoilte heard before the enormous splash was a voice shouting, *'This is all your fault . . .'*

Caoilte was the Running Man; the swiftest runner in all Erin, and one of its greatest, although now almost forgotten, heroes. He used his speed to trick dragons and outrun wild boars, and it was said that he could even race the wind.

The five-headed giant never came back to Erin. But it didn't drown; a creature like that couldn't drown. More than likely it was swept away on the waves, and is now marooned on some tiny island, where Dibh, Dubh, Damh, Dobh and Domh are still arguing.

The Slave

Not all the Irish kings were honourable men; some were thieves and bandits, a lot of them were pirates. Perhaps the most well known pirate-king was Niall of the Nine Hostages. He often raided the coasts of Britain and Gaul for slaves and booty, carrying both back to Erin in his longships.

Many of the slaves disappeared, and nothing more was ever heard of them. Some gained their freedom or fought in Erin's armies, and their names have been recorded in the ancient tales. But one particular slave became very famous . . .

I was born in the town of Bannavem Taberniae on the southwest coast of Britain. It was a small town, but, because it had a good harbour, it was both busy and wealthy. My father was the *decurion* — the tax collector — there. He was a Roman, and his name was Calpornius, and my mother was a princess of one of the western tribes of Britain. We lived in a villa on the edge of town and I can still remember how, in the summer and autumn evenings, when the sun dipped low in the sky, the white walls would burn red and gold in the light.

It was a summer evening like that when the raiders came. I was sitting on the beach watching the sun sink down into the sea, tossing pebbles into the white, foaming waves, when I saw the first black dots on the horizon.

I stood up and shaded my eyes, but they were still too far away to make out. They could only be ships, although

I knew that there were no ships due in harbour for the next few days, because my father had travelled south and east to Londinium on business, and he hadn't been expecting anything.

The sun sank lower in the skies, and the edge of it slipped down into the sea, the water sparkling bright with its colours. The ships were closer now and I began to make out the details. They were long thin craft, high in the bow — the front — and each one bore the beautifully carved figure of a dragon. They had huge square sails which were striped with red, blue or green. Along the sides of the craft were small round shields, and a row of long, thin oars stuck out on either side, making the ships look like giant insects dancing across the waves.

I didn't know what to do. I had never seen anything like them before, although the ships were something like those my father said the pirates from the land of Erin used. But what would they be doing this far from their own country?

I looked again, shading my eyes from the glare of the sun. And then I saw the reflection of the sun glinting and sparkling on the metal spears and swords, and the horned helmets of the men standing on the decks. On the ship closest to shore, a huge man suddenly stood up beside the carved dragon. He held a massive sword in one hand and a tall hunting spear in the other. His armour was a deep reddish bronze and his hair hung down his back in two thick knotted tails. He wore a thin bronze band around his head, which had a single emerald set in the front on his forehead.

I knew his name then. It could only be Niall of the Nine Hostages, King of the Land of Erin, the Pirate King.

I turned and ran up the beach, as hard and as fast as I could, slipping and sliding on the smooth stones. I shouted that the pirates had come, but at first the people only laughed at me, and thought I was joking. But then, when they saw how serious and frightened I was, they ran down to the harbour — just in time to see the first of the ships sail right up on to the beach, and the savage pirates come pouring out over the side.

The town was quite a small one, and there was no garrison of Roman soldiers as there were in some of the other towns, and, because it was late evening, the men coming home from the fields were exhausted and hardly had the energy to fight.

The pirates ran through the town and sealed off the two roads that led into it, trapping everyone within. And then they set about stealing what they could, going from shop to shop, from house to house, throwing everything they wanted out into the street, so that it could be collected later.

I crept along the back of the houses, making for our villa. I knew I could hide there, either in the cellars, or in the ice-house, which was a little way back from the house, where we stored milk and fruit and kept a fresh supply of ice all year round.

Once, I had to throw myself to the ground and roll under some bushes as some of the pirates ran past. They were all huge men, either with black or red hair and beards. They wore short leather jackets and some also wore a sort of leather or wool trousers. But most, of course, were dressed much as I was, in a short woollen tunic, belted around the waist, and with leather sandals. A lot of them wore gold rings around their upper arms, or had thick bracelets on their wrists, and some had beautifully carved and shaped pins holding their cloaks.

By the time I reached the villa, there was smoke rising from the town and I could smell burning wood. From the distance the villa looked untouched, but as I came nearer I saw that the main gates were open and the polished oak was cut and scarred, as if it had been cut with an axe or sword.

I hid in a little clump of bushes for a while and watched the house, but there was no movement, and that was strange. Nor were there any lights burning, even though the sun had now disappeared and night was fast approaching.

After a while, I slipped from the bushes and crept around the side of the house. As I rounded the building I saw the red glow of the burning town in the distance and a long line of white dots, which, I suddenly realised must be torches, heading down to the beach. The pirates would soon be away.

I climbed up the apple tree that grew outside the window of my room. I peered inside; it was so dark that I could see nothing, so I hung on the branch listening, but there was no sound from within.

At last I climbed in.

As far as I could see, my room was untouched and exactly as I had left it earlier that day. Crossing the floor as quietly as possible, I lifted the latch and peered out into the hall. With no lights it was difficult to see anything clearly, but from what I could see, nothing seemed to have been touched. Perhaps the pirates had missed the villa altogether, I thought.

However, I was half-way down the stairs when I heard the vague murmur of voices coming from the back of the house. I couldn't make out what they were saying, but it didn't sound like the rough, harsh language used by the pirates. It was then I realised that it was probably the servants, hiding in the cellars, waiting for Niall to lead his men away.

I hurried through the kitchens and down through the small doorway that led to the cellars. The voices stopped when they heard my sandals flapping down the stone steps. I pulled back the cellar door and quickly stepped inside. There was a light burning there, and I threw my hand up to shield my eyes.

'Marcus . . . ? Ladra . . . ?' I asked. The first was my father's head servant, and the second the cook.

Someone laughed.

Rough hands grabbed me from behind and I was hoisted up into the air. And then I saw that the cellar was full of the pirates. They were sorting through the stone jars that held my father's wine.

I was carried outside by a huge red-bearded pirate. He was laughing and said something to me in his strange language. I tried speaking to him in Latin and Greek and even tried the few words of Gaulish I knew, but he only continued laughing and shaking his head.

Once outside, he dropped me on the ground and tied a thick rope around my neck and then, leading me like some sort of animal, he set off towards the shore.

The beach was crowded, both with pirates and the townspeople. Most of them were tied up like me, but some had been set to work loading the pirates' longships with what they had stolen from the town.

When everything was loaded, the pirates began herding us on to the ships. It was now night and there was a full moon high in the heavens. It coloured the water silver and

black and for a moment, I thought perhaps that I was dreaming.

And then someone shoved me from behind, and I splashed into the icy water — and I knew that this was no dream.

I had been captured. I was now a slave of Niall of the Nine Hostages.

The boy was Patrick, later to become Saint Patrick, patron of Ireland. He spent many years in slavery in Erin before he escaped. However, he eventually returned to convert the pagan land to the Christian faith.

The Holy Bell

When Saint Patrick was travelling around Ireland, bringing the Word of God to the pagan people, he met the creature called An Chaorthanach or the Devil's Mother.

The Saint managed to banish her several times, but she always came back, and each time she was always more ugly and more dangerous. Like a cat, she had nine lives, and the last time, the ninth time, the saint met her was in the far west of Ireland . . .

The tall warrior leaned on his spear and pointed down the hill towards the dark waters of a lake. 'The creature's there in the lake,' he said in a whisper, almost as if he were afraid that it might hear him.

'Tell me what you know about it,' his companion said. The second man was small and darkly-tanned, with a hooked nose and dark eyes. He was wearing the simple brown robe of the followers of the New God, and he was called Patrick — although he was already beginning to be called a saint by the people.

'I haven't seen it myself,' Duban, the warrior, said. 'But I have seen the strange red and green light that glows beneath the surface of the water at night. I've also heard the strange shouts and roars that seem to be coming from up here when the moon is full. It's a terrible sound,' the young man shivered, remembering it, 'it's like a human in mortal terror, or a lost soul crying out for help.'

'Has anyone seen the creature in the lake?' Patrick asked softly. Although he spoke fluent Irish, he still had a touch of a strange accent from his childhood. Patrick had been brought to Erin as a slave from the Land of the Britons when he was only a child. He had spent many years herding pigs on the mountains in the north before an angel had helped him to escape. At first he had hated Erin and its people because they had made him a slave, but as he grew older he began to have dreams in which the Irish people were calling out for him to return. And so he had returned with the task of making Erin a Christian land and banishing the old dark gods.

'No one that I know of,' Duban said, and then he stopped. 'Hold on, there is someone . . .'

'Who?'

The warrior turned around and pointed out towards the seashore. 'Old Fergus lives in a cave on the beach,' he said. 'He is a strange man, half-mad it is said, but someone in the village said that Fergus has actually seen the creature.'

Patrick nodded his bald head. 'Well then, we will go and see this Fergus.'

Duban hesitated. The wind whipped his red hair into his eyes and pulled his cloak out behind him.

Patrick looked over at him. 'What's wrong?' he asked.

'The beach, although it looks close, is actually much further than it seems, and the track is very rough,' he said. 'I am a warrior, trained to march for long distances, but you . . .' He didn't finish the sentence.

The small man laughed, a rich gentle sound. 'For many years I lived on the side of a mountain, with only pigs for my companions. Their food and shelter were better than mine. I lived on what I could forage, I slept where I could. I've travelled on foot all across the lands of Europe, and I've walked from one end of this land to the other. I don't think a short walk is going to tire me out too much now, do you?' he smiled.

Duban smiled also, and shook his head. 'No, I suppose not.' He could see why so many people liked this man; he was so gentle and yet so strong at the same time, and he always seemed to be calm and confident. 'It's this way,' he said, and set off at a brisk walk towards the distant seashore.

They reached the beach close to evening, when the sun was low in the heavens, the light was beginning to fail, and the shadows beginning to darken. Fergus lived in a small cave set well back into the dark cliffs. They might have missed it had they not seen a thin thread of pale grey-white smoke drifting up lazily into the evening air from a small hole in the cliff. The opening to the cave was tiny, and both men had to crawl on hands and knees through a winding corridor of stone until it opened out into a single round room.

At first they thought that no one was there, although a small metal pot was bubbling softly on a tiny fire of turf and seaweed. From this came the smoke they had followed. The walls of the small, cramped cave had been painted with a white covering that looked and smelt faintly of bird droppings, and there were rushes and reeds scattered all across the floor. In one corner of the room, there was a bundle of fishing rods and lines and a tall spear leaned against a low three-legged stool.

And, except for a thick bundle of furs of all sorts and shapes and sizes thrown together in one corner, the room was empty.

'Where's Fergus?' Patrick asked his soft voice no louder than a whisper.

Duban laid down his spear and rested his sword on the floor beside him. He shrugged. 'I don't know, but he never strays far from his cave. Perhaps he's gone out for some weed or turf,' he suggested.

Patrick nodded, looking around the room. 'Aye, perhaps,' he said, sounding unconvinced. 'Perhaps.' Then he smiled. 'And then again, perhaps not. Perhaps Fergus heard two people crawling along the passage into his cave, and perhaps he hid. Eh?' he asked, suddenly yanking away one of the furs from the huge bundle.

A small grey-haired and grey-bearded head popped up, and looked at them with eyes the colour of fresh green grass. 'Perhaps he did,' the man said, in a high-pitched, sing-song voice. 'Perhaps he did.' He pushed off the furs and sat up, looking sharply at the two men. Behind his mass of hair and beard it was hard to make out his face, but Patrick got the impression of a round, wrinkled face, a button nose and a small mouth with no teeth.

'That's Fergus,' Duban said, relaxing and putting his sword back on to the floor. When the head had popped up, he had grabbed for the weapon.

'Fergus . . . Fergus . . . Fergus? Yes, I'm Fergus.' The old man said in his sing-song voice. He looked closely at Patrick and then he winked. 'You know, people say I'm mad — me!' he sounded so shocked and amazed that anyone could even think it, that Patrick had to smile.

'And are you mad?' he asked softly.

Fergus looked shocked. 'Of course I am! Anyone who lives in a cold, wet and smelly cave would want to be mad — and anyone who's seen half the things I've seen would certainly go mad.'

Patrick glanced across at Duban, and shook his head slightly, warning him to say nothing. He turned back to the old man. 'And what sort of things have you seen?' he asked gently.

Fergus shrugged his bony shoulders. 'Oh, all sorts. You see a lot of things here on the shore.'

'Tell me?' Patrick asked.

Fergus leaned forward and poked a long thin finger in the holy man's chest. 'I've seen islands floating in the sea. Islands with palaces, and islands with monsters, islands with walls of glass, islands with mountains of fire, islands with demons, islands . . .'

'Have you seen anything else — other than islands?' Patrick interrupted him.

Fergus looked disappointed that he couldn't finish his list of islands. 'Well, I've seen . . .' he paused and then lowered his voice to a whisper. 'I've seen demons. Have you ever seen a demon?' he asked Patrick.

The holy man nodded. 'Yes, many times.'

'Oh.' Fergus seemed surprised that anyone but himself could have seen a demon. 'Well, anyway, I'll bet I've seen a bigger demon than you.'

'How big was your demon?'

'Big.'

'How big?' Patrick asked casually.

'Very big.'

'As big as Duban here?'

'Oh, bigger,' Fergus smiled toothlessly. 'Much bigger.'

'As big as a boat?'

'Still bigger.' Fergus began to rock back and forth on his heels, enjoying himself. He began to mutter softly, and then to sing in a slightly scratchy voice. 'Oh, it was big, big, big, as big as a house, a house, a house.'

Patrick leaned forward and touched the old man on the knee. Fergus jumped with fright and looked at the holy man with wide frightened eyes. 'Tell me what it looked like,' Patrick said very gently.

'Ugly.'

'Tell me what it looked like,' Patrick said again.

'Ugly,' Fergus said. 'It looked like a frog, and it looked like a horse, and a pig and a cow.'

'Like a frog?' Patrick asked.

Fergus nodded his head quickly. 'Like a frog. A big, big, big fat frog, green and with warts, and huge round eyes.'

'Like a horse?'

The mad old man nodded again. 'Like a horse; she had a horse's ears and mane.'

Duban leaned over suddenly. 'Why did you say "*she*"?' he asked.

'Yes,' Patrick said, turning to Fergus, 'why did you call this creature a she?'

'Because she sang,' Fergus said, 'did I not say she sang?' he asked. And then, without waiting for a reply, he nodded. 'Oh yes, she sang with the voice of an angel.'

'And does she have a name?' Duban asked.

'Oh, everything has a name,' Fergus chanted, 'everything has a name, even I have a name. Have you a name?' he suddenly asked the holy man.

The saint nodded his bald head. 'My name is Patrick,' he said quietly, in his strange accent.

'Patrick, Patrick, Patrick,' Fergus said quickly, running the sound together until it sounded like *'patrickpatrick-patrick.'* And then he stopped, and looked at the holy man with his sharp bright eyes. 'Patrick the Holy Man? Patrick the Preacher? Patrick the Saint?'

'People have called me those names, but I am only a simple follower of the Christ God,' he said.

'Oh, I've heard of you. *She* told me about you.'

'She? Which she — surely not this she-demon with the angel's voice?'

Fergus nodded quickly. 'Yes, that she. She knows you; she's talked about you. She doesn't like you.' He finished and then he began laughing.

Patrick turned to Duban. 'Come on, let's get out of here. We've got what we came for.'

'Have we?' the warrior asked, puzzled. However, he turned and followed Patrick as they crept through the winding tunnel that led back to the fresh salt air of the beach. While they had been inside, night had fallen and the first of the night stars were beginning to sparkle and twinkle in the sky. There was a milky brightness low on the horizon where the moon would soon rise and the clouds close to it were coloured a pale silvery colour. Looking at them, Duban found it easy to believe the mad old man might believe that they were islands out there.

Patrick yawned and then stretched his arms wide. 'It's good to be back in the air again,' he said.

'Did you find out what you were looking for?' Duban asked.

'I think so. I can think of only one female demon with a sweet voice that should have reason to fear and hate me,' he said thoughtfully.

'Then you've met this creature before?'

Patrick nodded, and in the dim light his eyes sparkled with the reflected light of the stars. 'It must be *An Chaorthanach* — the Devil's Mother!'

The sun came up over the mountains and turned the dark waters of the lake gold and bronze in the light. There was silence for a few moments longer and then the morning birds began to sing — just one at first and then in small groups. They lined the branches of the trees and perched in the bushes, but strangely none would go near the lake, and no water bird floated on its still surface.

Patrick watched the birds carefully. While he had been a shepherd he had learned the ways of animals, and how they reacted. And he knew that animals could sense danger or evil. The holy man walked down to the water's edge and stared into the water. Nothing moved within; no fish swam beneath its surface, and he could see no tiny insects darting to and fro. The lake seemed to be dead.

He took a few steps back and then stooped down and picked up a handful of pebbles. Then, one by one, he tossed them out into the centre of the lake. They plopped into the water and the ripples began to spread.

'An Chaorthanach!' he called. 'Come out, I know you're there.'

But nothing happened.

'An Chaorthanach, come out — if you dare,' he added, with a cold smile.

For a few moments more nothing happened and he was just about to shout again, when the centre of the lake began to bubble and boil. The water turned white and frothing and then it began to push upwards. The whole lake was disturbed and little waves began to lap against the shore. All the birds suddenly took to the air, screaming and calling, and in a very short time, the air above the lake, and the trees and bushes about it were still and empty.

Patrick shivered suddenly, knowing something was about to happen.

And then An Chaorthanach rose up.

The lake bubbled and boiled and then a fountain of water shot up into the air, followed, almost immediately, by a huge creature that seemed to be all green warty flesh and huge staring eyes. Although the holy man had been expecting something like this he was still frightened — he had never seen anything so ugly in all his life.

An Chaorthanach was huge, and the part of her that was above the water was easily five times the height of a tall man. She was immensely fat, and seemed to be all wobbly green flesh. Her face was round and flat and there was a thick covering of coarse black hair on the top of her head and running down her back and a pair of huge pale pink ears poked up through this matted hair. There was something almost pig-like about her nose and mouth and she pawed the air with hooves that were similar to a cow's. Her wide saucer-like eyes swivelled around and fixed on the tiny man.

'Patrick,' she said softly, and her voice was like that of a young girl's, high and sweet and pure — but it sounded almost disgusting coming from that hideous creature.

'We meet again,' the holy man said, staring up at the demon. 'But I see you have chosen to assume your real shape this time,' he added.

The frog-creature's wide mouth opened in something like a smile, and a long black tongue shot out for a moment. 'I don't think we will ever meet again,' she said — and then she suddenly spat a tiny ball of fire towards the saint.

Patrick raised his stick, and struck the fireball, sending it high into the air where it exploded into a thousand tiny cold sparks.

Again and again, An Chaorthanach spat fire at the saint and again and again he managed to shield himself from

them. Soon the trees and bushes around them were burned and seared, and the grass was scarred with dark smouldering patches. A cloud began to form over the lake, a dark angry cloud made up out of tiny dust particles and pieces of ash and cinders, and the very air tasted sharp and bitter.

At last, An Chaorthanach began to tire and without saying a word, she slowly sank beneath the bubbling waters of the lake. Patrick leaned on his long stick, which was charred and smoking slightly. His eyebrows were singed and his cheeks, forehead and nose looked as if they had been sunburnt. The holy man was very tired. But he smiled to himself — if only the Devil's Mother knew how close she had come to winning!

However, Patrick knew that he couldn't win another battle with the creature. Next time she would kill him.

Patrick spent the next three days in prayer, asking God what he should do, wondering how he was going to defeat the monster that was slowly but surely killing all the farm animals and destroying the crops. He walked along the mountains, stopping in lonely places which always reminded him of his boyhood. Up there the air was fresh and clear — cold too — but Patrick was well used to the cold. He listened to the birds calling and the distant bleating of mountain sheep and goats and the whipping sound of the wind across the rocks. And then, on the third day, he heard another sound. A faint, very distant, but very sharp and penetrating sound — the sound of a church bell. And St Patrick had an idea.

It was almost ten days later before St Patrick returned to the dark lake. In that time he had spent his every waking hour with Athach, the blacksmith in the nearby village. In the first few days the small smithy was filled with the sounds of hammering and the roaring of bellows at all hours of the day and night — but no one thought to complain. They knew the saint was working on a plan to rid them of the creature — although they certainly hadn't got the faintest idea what it could be.

Duban came almost every day in a broad flat wagon pulled by two strong horses. And every day he carried in armloads of metal: old swords and spear heads, arrow tips, cracked shields, dented plates, rusted armour. Inside, Athach inspected every piece, picking some, and throwing the rest aside.

The huge blacksmith worked as he had never worked before, and Patrick worked alongside him. Although he was quite thin, the holy man was surprisingly strong, and he pumped the forge bellows from dawn to dusk with no signs of exhaustion — although it was a task that left even the blacksmith gasping for breath after only a few minutes' work. Six days passed and then two craftsmen arrived; one was small and stooped with a long grey beard and black, black eyes that seemed to be always darting and shifting and the other was a tall bald man with a round red face and soft brown eyes. The first was a worker in metal and the second a worker in leather.

Once they entered the smithy, Duban took up guard outside with his sword in his hand and instructions from Patrick to let no-one in — and no one out for that matter. Their meals were delivered to the door and Patrick himself came and brought them into the three men. The huge hammering and roaring of the bellows had stopped now and the only sounds were a lighter, almost musical metal-on-metal sound and a voice which sang softly to itself. But, besides these, there were no other sounds.

Three more days passed and then on the morning of the tenth day, just before the sun rose up over the horizon, the holy man quietly pulled back the door of the smithy. Duban, who was sleeping standing up, jerked awake at the tiny sound.

'Who . . . who's there?' he demanded, not yet fully awake.

'It's only me,' Patrick said softly. 'Now, quietly . . . let them sleep.' He glanced over his shoulder at the three sleeping men, the huge smith and the two craftsmen. 'They have worked hard — harder than they have ever worked in their lives, and they have worked for no reward, no payment.'

'What were you working on?' Duban asked, yawning widely. This was the morning of the tenth day he had been standing guard, and he was very tired.

'This,' Patrick said, and showed the young warrior a small leather satchel. It was only a bag, but beautifully made from the finest, softest leather and there was an ancient Celtic design on the cover twisting around a Christian Cross.

'It's beautiful,' Duban whispered, 'but what is it?'

But the saint only smiled and shook his head. 'Later,' he said. 'Come, we're going to the lake.'

At this early hour, the waters of the lake were dark and gloomy, and the night mist still hung low over the surface, giving it a very ghostly, sinister appearance. With the burnt trees, withered bushes, and the blackened grass, it looked very much as Duban imagined Hell would look like.

'You stay here,' Patrick said, when they were close to the water. 'And on no account are you to let the creature see you. I can protect myself — I cannot protect you. Do you understand?' he asked sharply.

The warrior nodded without saying a word. He felt quite frightened now. It was one thing to face warriors in battle but quite another to face the Devil's Mother.

Patrick marched down to the water's edge and stuck his staff into the soft earth. 'An Chaorthanach,' he called. 'I have come for you!'

There was no waiting this time, and the water in the centre of the lake immediately bubbled and frothed and the mist shifted and swirled like angry storm clouds and then the horrible figure of An Chaorthanach loomed up, her huge eyes staring and her black forked tongue flickering.

'There is no escape now, holy man,' she said in her sweet girl's voice. She spat a ball of fire at the saint, and then another and then another.

Patrick lifted his right hand and made a sign of the cross in the air. For a single moment it glowed a pale blue-white and then the balls of fire struck it. The air was suddenly filled with a buzzing, hissing, sparking sound, and there was a terrible smell of burning. For a few heartbeats the glowing blue cross and the balls of cold red fire crackled together in the air around the saint and then they disappeared.

Patrick smiled. 'You see, my God protects me.'

An Chaorthanach screamed aloud, a long, high terrible scream that echoed and re-echoed across the water and through the still air for miles and everyone who heard it fell to their knees and prayed — either to the New Christian God or their old Pagan gods.

'I am going to crush you,' she suddenly shouted, and then, slowly, very slowly, An Chaorthanach began to make her way through the lake towards the man. The water boiled and hissed and dirty waves lapped at Patrick's feet. But the creature was so big and bulky that she made little headway through the water and so she sank beneath the surface with the intention of swimming in close to the shore and then surfacing.

And this was what the holy man had been waiting for.

He had very little time, he knew. On land, or the surface of the water, An Chaorthanach was slow and clumsy, but beneath the waves, she was sleek and fast, like a seal. He ran to the water's edge and sank to his knees in the soft earth. With his small rough hands, he slipped the knots on the leather satchel and pulled out a small metal object. He held it high in the air in both hands before lowering it to the surface of the water . . . and then he waited.

Duban parted the leaves of a bush and stared at the object the saint was holding in his hand. It was metal, and beautifully worked, he could see that, and the design

etched into the metal was the work of a master craftsman. The warrior shook his head; but what was it? Just what was it? It looked like . . . it looked like . . .

It looked like a bell!

It *was* a bell; a small, metal hand-bell. Duban had expected many things — a sword, a knife, even a magical wand, but certainly not a bell. Had the holy man gone mad? What use was a bell against a terrifying monster like the Devil's Mother?

There was movement beneath the surface, and a long v–shaped wave was moving towards the saint. Patrick bowed his head for a moment, and then slowly, slowly, slowly, he lowered the bell into the water. Duban could see his hand moving to and fro as he rang the bell . . .

For a few pounding heartbeats nothing happened, and Duban thought the saint's plan had failed. And then with a terrifying crack, the water of the lake froze into a solid sheet of stone!

And Chaorthanach was trapped. Workmen came from the village later that day and began to break up the stones from the lake. The women in the village then pounded them into dust, and the dust was thrown out over the sea. An Chaorthanach was no more.

Saint Patrick moved on, taking his magical bell with him. When he eventually died, many, many years later, new craftsmen worked on it, and they made a special box for it from gold and silver and precious stones, and with the most marvellous and beautiful designs worked into the metal. It was called a bellshrine.

And the Shrine of Saint Patrick's Bell survives today.

Hero

When we think of heroes we think of brave knights on horseback, wearing armour and carrying spears and swords. They do battle with demons and dragons, evil knights and magicians.

But there are other kinds of heroes; heroes we never hear about . . .

Etan and Ronan ducked down behind the bushes when they heard the sound of the horses approaching. These were dangerous times they were living in and you had to be very careful of strangers.

Ronan carefully parted a few leaves and peered out, down the dry, dusty road that led through the woods towards the lake. For a few moments he saw nothing, and then he spotted a cloud of white dust in the distance, moving through the trees along the road.

'Who is it?' Etan, his sister whispered.

Ronan shook his head. 'I can't see yet; they're still too far away.' Ronan was ten, just one year younger than Etan. They both had coal-black hair and large dark eyes, set in long faces, and they looked very alike.

'Can you see anything yet?' Etan demanded.

'No . . .' Ronan began, but then said, 'Yes; it's all right, I can see Niall. He must be returning with the King's men.'

The boy and girl stepped out of the bushes and stood by the side of the road, waiting for the warriors to draw closer. If they were lucky they might be able to get a ride on one of the horses back to their father's fort. Ronan and Etan were the children of Dalbach, Lord of the O'Byrne clan, and he owned most of the land in this part of the country.

The riders were nearer now and the children could see that something was very wrong indeed. For a start, there didn't seem to be half as many of them as had gone out that morning, and the few that remained were all battered and bloodied, and their armour was torn and filthy. Many of them had lost their weapons, and none were carrying their tall spears. Some swayed in their saddles and had to be held by other riders, and there were a few who were so badly wounded that they were unable to ride, and had to be tied across their saddles like sacks of grain, with their arms and legs dangling.

The leader of the riders, Niall, raised his hand and called the rest to a halt when he spotted the wide-eyed, open-mouthed children. Niall was their father's brother and he also commanded the O'Byrne clan's small force of soldiers. The tall man was pale and there was a rough bandage tied around his head, and one of his eyes was so bruised that it was almost shut.

'What happened?' Ronan asked in a whisper.

'The beast attacked us,' Niall said, his voice harsh and croaking. 'Come on now, this is no time to be playing in these woods — the thing may be after us. We have to reach the fort before dark.'

'But what happened to the rest of the men?' Etan asked, as Niall gripped her arm and pulled her up on to the horse in front of him. 'Where are they?'

'We are all that are left,' Niall said sadly, looking back at the small group of warriors behind him. He reached down and pulled Ronan up behind him. 'Hold tight now,' he said.

'But about twenty men went out this morning,' Ronan said in amazement.

Niall nodded. 'Twenty-two men to be exact,' he said.

Ronan looked over his shoulder, and did a quick count. 'There are only ten men and you left.'

'But I thought you were going to kill the beast,' Etan said in astonishment. 'Father said that it didn't stand a chance.'

'And you had some of the king's men with you also,' Ronan added.

'I know,' Niall said wearily. 'But we were wrong, and now there are eleven good men dead and devoured because of our mistake.'

'What is father going to say?' Ronan wondered as Niall raised his hand and nudged his horses into a trot.

Niall sighed and shook his head. 'I wish I knew . . .'

Dalbach stood with his back to the huge roaring fire and listened silently to his brother's story. The large room was filled with people, mostly Dalbach's own warriors, but some from the High King's court at Tara. Servants moved around quietly, clearing the long table, and filling the large cups with mead.

' . . . and that's what happened,' Niall finished. 'We never had a chance. I've never seen anything so fast in all my life.' He took a quick swallow from the cup in his hand.

'Describe the creature,' Dalbach said softly. He was a short, rather stout man, almost ten years older than his brother. His hair, which had once been as dark as his children's, was now thin and grey, and his thick, bushy beard was also streaked with grey threads. There were lines on his forehead, and under his eyes, and at this moment, he looked very old indeed.

'It was big,' Niall said, 'long and slender, with huge eyes . . .' He shook his head, 'I can't remember anything else it all happened so fast . . .'

Ronan and Etan pushed the door open very gently. They had been listening to Niall's tale through the door, but now they had to open it because their uncle's voice had grown so soft. They were both shivering in their long night robes, even though they had thrown heavy furs over their shoulders. They couldn't come into the warm room because they had been sent to bed earlier.

'What's he saying?' Etan whispered in her brother's ear.

'*Sssh*, listen,' he murmured.

' . . . it all happened so fast. One moment the lake was smooth and calm, and the men were setting up their weapons, and the next the water just erupted up and out and then this thing appeared.' Niall shook his head. 'It was terrible, terrible. We didn't stand a chance.'

Dalbach nodded and then rested his hands on his brother's shoulders. Both of them had known all the men who had died for many years. They had grown up with them; they had been their friends.

'What do we do now sir?' someone in the room asked.

Dalbach straightened up. 'Well, we've tried force of arms, now I'm afraid we must try magic.'

A quick murmur ran around the room. The land of Erin was now Christian — there were some parts which still followed the old pagan faith, but magic was now frowned upon.

'I can't agree with that,' a rasping, harsh voice at the back of the room said, and all heads turned to look at the tall thin man in the simple brown robe of a monk.

'I don't agree with magic myself, Brother Colman,' Dalbach said, 'but I have no choice. There is an Oillpeist — a dragon-worm — living in a lake on my land. It has destroyed crops, uprooted trees, turned valuable land into waste ground, and lately it has started killing the animals. And now . . . well, you saw for yourself what it did today.' Dalbach shook his head firmly. 'I cannot allow it to go on.'

'But there must be some other way,' Brother Colman said, folding his arms and staring at the older man.

'Then tell me what it is and I will use it,' Dalbach snapped. 'No, Brother Colman, you know I am a Christian, and follow the True Faith and my children have been baptised as Christians also, but in this case there is nothing I can do.'

'It is a sin,' Brother Colman retorted.

'Probably,' Dalbach murmured, and then he looked at one of the servants. 'Bring the wise woman in.'

'I cannot allow this,' Brother Colman began.

'You cannot stop it,' Niall said.

'You — *you* are the king's man, you stop it,' Brother Colman said, turning to a hugely muscled man who was standing to one side of the fire. He was Fergal, commander of the king's men. When Dalbach had sent to Tara for help, the king had sent him Fergal with a squad of men to help destroy the Oillpeist. But now three of his own men were dead, and over half of them wounded.

Fergal looked at Brother Colman with his ice-blue eyes, and then he slowly shook his head. 'I would do exactly the same.'

'Then I will tell the king,' Brother Colman said loudly.

'And he will laugh at you,' Fergal said with a smile. 'He may follow the new faith, but he still has respect for the old ways.'

Brother Colman opened his mouth to say something and then seemed to think better of it. He turned on his heel and walked towards the door.

Ronan and Etan saw him coming and had to make a dash for the darkest shadows. They huddled together and held their breath as the door was flung open and a long bar of light was thrown out across the hall. Then Brother Colman stepped into the light and slammed the door shut behind him. The two children remained still for a few moments longer as the holy man's hard-soled sandals clattered down along the stone floor. At last they heard another door slam and they knew he had gone into his room. With a sigh of relief they darted back to the door, and pressed their ears against the cold wood. They could hear their father speaking.

'. . . and this is Fand; she is a wise woman and she has agreed to help us.'

There was a dry cackling laugh and then an almost rusty sounding voice spoke. 'I'm what that brown-robed one would call a witch. But he would only call me that because he's frightened of me. He forgets that his own Saint Patrick used magic when he needed to.'

Ronan and Etan pressed the door open a space and peered in. They saw a small old woman sitting before the fire with her hands wrapped around a large cup of mead. She was dressed mostly in strips of animal furs which had been sewn together into a huge shapeless dress and there was a cloak which had also been made up out of animal skins thrown over her shoulders. Her face looked like an apple — an old dry wrinkled apple, but her eyes were bright, very bright and piercing. The two children couldn't make out the colour of her eyes from the distance, although they did look to be a sort of reddish shade.

'We need your help old woman,' Dalbach began.

'Oh, I know, I know,' Fand cackled again, and smiled, and both children were amazed to see that she still had all her own teeth.

'How do we get rid of the Oillpeist?' he asked.

'You feed it,' Fand said, with another grin.

'Feed it?' Niall asked.

The old woman nodded. 'Aye, you feed it.'

'Do you mean poison it?'

Fand laughed again, long and hard, and everyone there felt shivers running up and down their spines with the eerie sound. 'Yes, you might say that.'

'If you tell me what sort of bait or poison you need I can send to Tara for it,' Fergal said.

The old woman took a quick drink from her cup.'Oh, I would imagine you would have the bait here.'

'Well, what is it?' Dalbach asked impatiently.

'Watch,' Fand said. She reached in under her cloak and then pulled out a small leather bag which was held shut by a string pulled through the top. Holding the bag in one hand, and with the cup of mead in the other, she pulled it open with her teeth. Then she set it down on her knees and, reaching in she took out a tiny pinch of white powder.

'Watch,' she said again, and she threw the powder on the fire.

Everyone held their breath, expecting to see something happen, expecting fire and sparks to go shooting around the room, or perhaps different coloured flames to go leaping high into the air. But nothing like that happened. People were just beginning to murmur amongst themselves, when they suddenly noticed that the fire had gone very dull, and there seemed to be a lot more smoke than usual. But this smoke, instead of drifting away up the chimney, hung in a solid mass just above the burning logs.

'Watch,' Fand said for the third time, and now colours began to coil and twist through the solid mass of grey smoke. The colours shifted and turned, bent and looped and soon the grey disappeared and was replaced by a shifting ball of light.

'Now look,' the old woman said, and suddenly all the shifting, twisting, coiling colours seemed to come together and then a great gasp went around the room as a picture formed in the ball. A picture of a small blue lake, surrounded by trees, with a bright blue sky with white clouds overhead. A moving picture, with birds darting across the sky, and the waters of the lake rippling in the breeze.

Everyone was watching the magic so closely that Ronan and Etan risked creeping into the room and snuggling down behind one of the tables which had been pushed into a corner. Now they could see everything clearly.

'I know that lake,' Etan said suddenly, her breath tickling Ronan's ear.

He nodded. 'So do I. It's the one we're not supposed to go near, the one where the Oillpeist lives.'

His older sister nodded. She was staring intently at the magical picture, and then she frowned. 'What's that?' she said, and her voice sounded so strange that Ronan quickly looked from her to the fire.

He saw then what had startled Etan. The picture had grown, or perhaps they had somehow come even closer to

the lake, because they were now very close to the water's edge, and they could see the burn and scorch marks on the earth, and the uprooted trees and seared bushes where the Oillpeist had crawled up out of the water. There was an old tree stump there. Whatever tree it had once held had long since fallen into the water and disappeared. The ragged stump had once been the children's favourite spot for sunbathing or fishing. It was perfectly flat and, even on the coolest day, it was always warm.

Now however, it was burnt and blackened where the Oillpeist had breathed on it, but it was not that which had upset his sister. Tied to the ancient tree stump was Etan herself! In the picture she was dressed all in white and had a slim golden crown around her head. Her hair, which was usually tied up, was now loose and flowed down her back, and she seemed to be sleeping.

And then the waters of the lake bubbled and boiled and suddenly a huge head rose up through the mist, and two flat, slit-pupilled eyes swivelled to look at the girl, and then the massive head swooped . . . and the picture dissolved as a gust of wind blew through the room, disturbing the smoke.

Etan buried her head in her brother's shoulder to stop herself from screaming. Ronan could hear her heart thumping against his chest, and he knew his own pulse was racing. He wasn't sure what he had just seen or what it meant, but he had a very bad feeling about it.

'Would you care to explain this . . . this image,' Dalbach asked, his voice barely above a whisper. He too had been disturbed by what the old woman had shown him, but he also had an inkling of what it meant.

'I would have thought you knew,' Fand cackled. 'To kill the Oillpeist, you must first feed it a young girl. A Christian girl should do very nicely.' She paused and then added, 'And of course, she must have some royal blood in her.'

'But this is monstrous,' Dalbach protested, 'we cannot just sacrifice a human being to this creature.'

Fand nodded, agreeing. 'No, not just a human being; a girl, a royal-blooded, Christian girl. The Oillpeist will touch no other meat.'

'Will it poison him?' Fergal asked softly.

Fand shrugged her bony shoulders. 'All I know is that it never fails.'

'Never?'

'Never,' Fand said.

Fergal turned back to Dalbach. 'Well?' he asked.

'Well what? Surely you don't expect me to . . .' He stopped when he saw the look in the other man's eyes. 'You do, don't you? You expect me to kill a young girl . . .'

'A Christian, royal-blooded girl,' Fand reminded him.

'What will happen if the creature isn't destroyed?' Fergal suddenly asked the old woman.

'At the moment it's still very small . . .'

'But it's huge!' Niall protested.

'It is still growing,' Fand continued. 'In another year or so it will be fully grown, and then . . .' she shrugged.

'And then?' Fergal asked.

Fand smiled. 'And then it will be able to destroy this fort as easily as you or I crack an egg.' The old woman laughed. 'It will then go on a rampage across the country, destroying everything in its path.'

'In what direction?' Fergal asked.

'East of course,' Fand said, 'all Oillpeists head towards the east, I don't know why.'

'But Tara lies to the east,' Fergal said in alarm.

'Then tell your king to move now,' the old woman began to laugh then, cackling and coughing until the tears streamed down her face.

Some servants came in and took the old woman away, but everyone could still hear her shrill laughter echoing down along the corridors for a long time afterwards.

'There was a girl in the picture,' Fergal said at last, 'who was she?'

Dalbach shrugged. 'I don't know,' he said quickly.

Fergal grinned. 'I don't believe you,' he said slowly. 'I was watching you when she appeared, aye, and you also Niall. You both know the girl — now who is she?' he demanded.

'She is my daughter,' Dalbach said eventually.

'She is a Christian? She has royal blood in her veins?'

Dalbach nodded miserably.

'Even so, she must be given to the Oillpeist.'

'Never; you'll have to kill me first.'

'If you do not send your daughter to the creature, I will have to ride on to Tara and tell the king what has happened here. Then he will come here with an army; he will destroy your fort, make slaves of all your people, kill you and all your family and *then* send your daughter to the creature. So you have a choice . . .'

'A choice?' Dalbach shouted. 'What choice do I have?'

Dalbach came to the children's room just before the sun rose the following morning. They were both awake — indeed, they hadn't slept all night — and were sitting up in bed waiting for him when he eased open the door and peeked inside. He was a little surprised at finding them both awake at this early hour — usually they were almost impossible to get up in the morning.

'Oh, I didn't think you would be awake yet,' he said softly, stepping into the room.

Etan and Ronan just looked at him and said nothing.

'Something has happened,' Dalbach said very slowly, 'something terrible . . .'

'We know, father,' Ronan said quietly, 'we heard.'

'But how did you hear?' he asked in astonishment. 'Only a few people know at the moment.'

'We were listening last night,' Etan said, 'we heard everything.'

Dalbach sat down on the edge of Etan's bed and buried his head in his hands. 'I don't want to do it,' he said, and his voice sounded rough and hoarse.

'I know,' Etan whispered, although her own voice sounded tight and her throat was burning.

'But I've got no choice,' Dalbach continued, as if he hadn't heard her. 'If we don't kill the Oillpeist, then it will grow up and ravage the country. If I don't give you to the creature, then the High King will come with his army and destroy us and then he will give you to the Oillpeist anyway. What do I do?'

Dalbach sounded so lost and lonely that Etan rested her head against his back and wrapped her arms around his shoulders. Ronan got up out of his bed and knelt on the floor beside his father. 'Don't worry,' he whispered, 'we've got a plan.'

'What use is a plan against a creature like the Oillpeist?'

'When . . . when do I . . . I go to the . . . the Oillpeist?' Etan asked slowly.

Dalbach stood up and looked at both his children. His eyes were bright and shining, and he seemed to have aged many years in the single night. 'This morning; you go to the creature this morning,' he whispered, and then turned and hurried from the room.

A sad and silent procession wound its way down along the white track that led into the forest and to the lake. Dalbach and Niall rode at the front, with Ronan and Etan behind them on their own small ponies. Behind them came Fergal with the rest of the warriors, and behind these, most of the servants from the fort. No one said anything and even the sounds of the forest, the chirpings of the birds, the crackling of the leaves and branches as the smaller animals pushed their way through the undergrowth, seemed to be missing. Even the very air seemed to be still — still and waiting.

Etan was dressed exactly as she had been in Fand's magical moving image. She was wearing a long white robe of the finest material, which had an ancient Celtic pattern in rich gold thread running along the hem, the neck and the cuffs of the sleeves. There was a simple golden metal band resting on her rich dark hair, which, this morning, had been brushed until it shone, and allowed to flow down her back. Etan was pale, and her eyes were red-rimmed, but she rode her pony steadily enough.

Ronan trotted his animal along beside her. He had often fought with his sister — what brother and sister didn't? — but he had to admire her now, she was so calm and yet she knew she was almost certainly going to her death in the jaws of a terrible creature.

Soon the trees thinned out and the riders spotted the blue water of the lake. The track led downwards now and then twisted around two huge trees and out on to a rough stony shore. Here everyone stopped, and stared at the lake.

The lake was not large, but it was supposed to be bottomless. A deep underground river connected it to another lake further west and this, in turn, led down to the sea. The water itself was very dark and almost dirty-looking because all the land around the lake was bog-land and the peat seeped into the water, colouring it. It was exactly the sort of lake an Oillpeist might choose to live in.

'Quickly now,' Fergal said, riding up behind Dalbach, Etan and Ronan, 'we don't have much time. Where's this tree stump we saw last night?'

Ronan pointed off to one side to where a clump of trees and bushes came down almost to the water's edge. They were all crushed and burnt, and the earth all around them was torn and scarred as if some huge beast had pulled itself up by its claws.

Dalbach looked at his daughter. 'You don't have to go, you know that?' he whispered. 'I'll fight for you — I'd fight the High King for you.'

'But the Oillpeist is still growing,' Etan whispered. 'What will happen in a few years' time when it is destroying the countryside? I can prevent that from happening.'

Dalbach kissed his daughter on the forehead. 'Your mother would have been very proud of you,' he whispered. The children's mother Almu had died when Ronan had been only a few days old, and they had never known her, although everyone spoke of her as being a lovely, kind woman, whom Etan was not unlike in looks.

Fergal then took Etan by the hand and walked her down to the edge of the water and the tree stump. He produced a length of rope and quickly looped it around her waist and then on to the scorched tree stump.

'It's not very tight,' Etan said.

Fergal smiled sadly. 'I know you must think very badly of me, but I have a daughter of my own about your age; I know how hard this must be for Dalbach. But you know it has to be done, don't you?'

Etan nodded.

Fergal finished tying the knot and stepped back, and then he suddenly pulled his sword free — and saluted Etan as if she were a queen! 'You are a very brave young lady,' he said quietly, and then he stepped back from the tree stump and marched up the beach.

'What do we do now?' Dalbach asked, hardly able to look at the small figure of his daughter tied to the blackened tree stump by the water's edge.

'Now we wait,' Fergal said.

They waited on into the morning, but nothing happened. The sun rose in the heavens and crept across the sky and the shadows on the ground grew shorter and shorter, until they had almost disappeared . . .

At exactly midday, the Oillpeist appeared.

At first there was just a ripple on the surface of the water — a simple ripple as if a stone had been dropped in. And then the ripple grew and grew, spreading out from the centre of the lake in ever-growing circles. Then, large bubbles began appearing on the surface of the lake. These bubbles burst with quick, sharp pops and left a foul odour on the air.

Everything had now become very silent indeed, and the noise from the lake seemed even louder than it actually was.

The water in the centre of the lake began to boil and yellow-white froth appeared. More and more boiled up and then when the centre of the lake was in turmoil, a head appeared.

The Oillpeist's head was huge.

The head was long and flat, with two huge cat-like eyes set on either side of a bony ridge that ran down the centre of its face and formed a bird-like beak, jutting out behind its head like a single backward horn. The head was attached to a long, almost slender-looking neck that, in turn, was connected to a long, long body, that was covered with hard black scales. There were six legs, each one ending in three massive talons, and the tail that broke the surface of the water and waved in the air was studded with spiky bones.

The Oillpeist's evil-looking head waved to and fro, as if it were looking for something, and two tendrils of grey smoke drifted from its nostrils. Suddenly it spotted Etan. It swooped . . .

. . . and stopped before her, its huge eyes wide and unblinking, and with just the tip of a forked tongue flickering between its lips.

Etan pulled as far away from the creature as possible, but, although Fergal had tied her loosely, she was still secure. She turned her head away and took a deep breath — the smell was terrible.

And then, the Oillpeist lifted its huge head, opened its mouth and roared. The sound was so powerful that it knocked everyone to the ground; horses reared up and galloped off into the forest, and the lake was churned to a frenzy. A huge spout of flame shot out from the Oillpeist and curled into the air. Luckily most of it fell back on to the water, and that which fell on to the land quickly burned itself out.

And then, the Oillpeist's head twisted down and it opened its huge mouth . . .

Etan saw its hundreds of massive yellowed teeth, and its long black tongue in its raw red mouth, and she squeezed her eyes shut and said a final prayer . . .

Someone moved in the bushes by her side. It was Ronan. With a scream that was almost as terrifying as the Oillpeist's, he dashed from his hiding place, swinging something over his head. As he neared his sister, he let it go and it sailed through the air, straight down the creature's throat . . .

The Oillpeist closed his mouth with surprise and then it opened it to roar and spit flame at him. Smoke trickled out and then there was a muffled *whump* as the Oillpeist's head was engulfed in flame. It reared up screaming as the flames burnt through it. Now there were flames coming from its mouth and nose and ears. It threshed its head around, trying to shake off the fire, but it was too late. With a final scream, the Oillpeist slumped down onto the stony beach by Etan's feet. It was dead.

The girl opened one eye and then looked at her brother. 'It worked,' she said with a sigh of relief.

'Of course it worked; I told you it would.'

'But you might have been wrong,' Etan said with a smile, 'and where would I have been then?'

Dalbach came running up. He was laughing and crying at the same time, and he fell to his knees and hugged his two children. 'What did you throw at it?' he finally asked Ronan.

The boy smiled. 'A jug of fish-oil.'

The Oillpeist usually spat out a long streamer of flame, but when it had bitten down on the jug Ronan had thrown into its mouth, the oil had spread everywhere, and so, when the Oillpeist had spat fire again, the inside of its mouth had caught light!

Ronan had defeated the Oillpeist where everyone else had failed. He was a hero. But he never did any other heroic deed; he grew up to be a farmer, and Etan was married to one of the western lords. But people still remember Ronan; they never forget a hero . . .

The Human Hounds

Finn was amongst the greatest of the old Irish heroes. He was a mighty warrior who, with the Knights of the Fianna, kept law and order in the land. He had many friends both in this world and in the fairyland, but his constant companion and most trusted friend was his huge war-hound, Bran.

Bran was a magical beast, stronger, faster and more intelligent than any normal dog, and in a strange roundabout way, he was actually related to Finn . . .

Tuirean was Finn's aunt; she was his mother's youngest sister, and not much older that Finn himself. She was a young woman of astonishing beauty, with long, coal–black hair that reached to the back of her knees, a small round face, and huge dark eyes. Many young men fell in love with her and asked for her hand in marriage, but she always turned them down.

Now one day, Tuirean met a man called Illan, one of Finn's captains from the north, and she fell in love with him immediately. He was tall and handsome, and his hair, like Tuirean's was coal-black, and he had fallen in love with the small bright-eyed beauty the first time they met. But, because Illan was under Finn's command, he had to ask his permission to marry Tuirean.

Finn, Illan and the rest of the Fianna had been out hunting a gang of thieves who had been stealing from the villages. Around noon they had stopped on the bank of the river Boyne to eat their lunch and wait for the scouts to bring them news of the gang. Illan walked over to Finn and sat down beside him, resting his plate on his knee. 'I've something to ask you,' he said.

Finn, who was dangling his hot feet in the water, looked up. He was a tall, thin young man, with dark brown hair and the beginnings of a beard. But you could tell by his eyes that he was very wise, for they were the eyes of an old, old man. 'What would you like to ask me?' he said.

'I would like permission to marry,' Illan said softly, blushing slightly.

Finn smiled. He had seen Illan with his aunt over the past few weeks and he had guessed that this might happen. 'Would I know the lady?' he asked innocently.

'Aye,' Illan nodded, 'it is your own mother's sister, Tuirean.'

'My aunt,' Finn said.

Illan nodded. 'Your aunt. I love her you see,' he continued, 'and we wish to be married as soon as possible. And because you are my commander and since the girl's father — your grandfather — is no longer alive, I thought I should ask you.' He paused and added, 'What do you say?'

Finn pulled his feet up out of the water and began to dry them on the edge of his cloak. He glanced over at the older man. 'What if I should say no?' he asked.

The smile faded from Illan's face. 'Well,' he said uncomfortably, 'if you were to say no, then I suppose we would just run away and get married anyway. But I hope you won't say no,' he said.

Finn stood up and Illan scrambled to his feet. He put his hand on Illan's shoulder and the young man smiled warmly. 'Of course I wouldn't say no, and of course you may marry her — but only on one condition,' he added.

'What's that?' Illan asked.

'If I find that you are not good to my aunt, or that she does not like living in your fort, then you will allow her to return at once.'

Illan smiled. 'I will always be good to your aunt, and don't worry, I will be sending a messenger to my fort today with instructions to prepare it for my wife.'

Finn laughed and then shook Illan's hand in both of his. 'I hope you will both be very happy together,' he said.

'I know we will be,' Illan said.

Even as they were speaking, the scouts returned. They had come across fresh tracks further down the river and they had also discovered the remains of a camp-fire, which meant that the thieves were only an hour or so ahead of the Fianna. Finn hopped into his sandals while Illan ran off to gather up his belongings and pack them onto the back of his horse. Soon the Knights of the Fianna galloped off down along the banks of the river Boyne after the gang. Illan couldn't resist laughing out loud. If they caught the thieves today, he could be back home by midday tomorrow and he and Tuirean could begin preparations for their wedding.

The day wore on. Finn and the Fianna always seemed to be just a little behind the thieves, and once they even saw them in the distance just riding over a hill. The Fianna had galloped after them, but by the time they reached the hill, there was a thin column of smoke rising from behind it, and when they rode over the crest, they found that the thieves had burned the bridge across a deep and rushing river. The Fianna were then forced to ride five miles upriver to find a spot where they could cross over without any risk of being swept away, and of course, by that time, the gang had disappeared.

They spent that night in a small forest not far from the sea shore. As well as the rich damp smell of the forest, there was also the tangy salt smell of the sea. Finn posted guards, because the forests then were dark and dangerous places, with gangs of bandits and packs of wolves roaming through them.

Illan was one of the guards. He picked a spot a little away from the roaring camp fire in a thick clump of bushes, where he would be able to see anyone or anything approaching, but remain hidden.

Back in the camp someone took out a harp and began to sing along to it, and Illan recognised the delicate voice of Cnu Derceol, Finn's favourite singer, who had learned to sing in the fairy forts of the *Sidhe*. The men fell silent, listening to the beautiful voice, and slowly the night creatures in the forest stopped their creakings and croakings and twitterings to listen to the voice, and Illan saw more than one pair of small round eyes staring out of the trees and bushes towards the fire.

The night wore on, and the fire died down to glowing embers, flaky grey pieces of wood crumbling every now and again to send tiny red sparks spiralling up into the night sky. Soon, the only noises were the nightsounds of the forest, the gentle hissing of the sea and the snoring of the men in the camp.

Illan was tired. It had been a long day, and he had ridden far, and he was eager to return home to tell Tuirean that they could be married. He hadn't really thought that Fionn would refuse — but at least he had agreed without an argument, and everything was all right now. He began to wonder what it would be like to be married . . .

Something white moved through the trees. Illan caught his breath and stiffened, and slowly, very slowly, he pulled out his sword. He waited, trying to follow the movements of the white shape through the trees. He wasn't sure what it was — but he was not going to call the camp awake until he was sure. He remembered when he was a young man shouting the alarm, and it turned out to be nothing more than fog weaving through the tree trunks.

The shape came nearer. Illan was nearly sure now that it was a figure — a human figure — but something stopped him from calling the alarm. Suddenly the shape seemed to melt into the ground, and then someone spoke from behind him.

'Hello Illan.'

He spun around, bringing his sword up to defend himself, but it got tangled in the bushes' thorny branches and fell from his hands. The pale woman standing before him laughed merrily.

'Dealba!' he said in astonishment.

The young woman smiled, showing her small, sharp teeth. 'So you do remember me,' she said softly, her voice sounding as ghostly as the wind.

'Of course I remember you,' Illan said, 'how could I ever forget you?' He shivered a little then, because Dealba frightened him, and Illan Eachta was afraid of neither man nor beast, but he did fear the fairy-folk — and Dealba was one of the *Sidhe* folk. She was a banshee, a fairy woman.

Illan had met her a few years ago, when he had been doing coast-guard duty, watching the shores for any signs of pirates, or bandits attempting to land on Erin's coasts. They had met one stormy winter's night, when the seas had been pounding in over the beach, sending foam high into the sky, roaring and crashing like a hungry animal. When Illan had seen the white woman moving up the beach he had thought she was a ghost, but it was not until she was closer did he realise that she was just one of those very pale people that he sometimes saw in the king's court, and her white clothing made her seem even paler. They had become friends of a sort then; coast-guard was a lonely duty and Dealba was someone to talk to and laugh with. And it was not until later that he learned that she was one of the fairy women — the terrible banshee.

Illan suddenly realised that Dealba was speaking. 'I'm sorry,' he said, 'what did you say?'

Dealba frowned. 'I said that I heard that you have a new woman in your life now.'

Illan nodded. 'Yes, her name is Tuirean, and we will be married soon.'

'And what about me?' Dealba asked.

Illan shook his head. 'What do you mean?' he asked.

'I thought we would be married one day?' she said. 'You told me so yourself,' she reminded him.

'Yes, but that was before I knew you were one of the *Sidhe*. You know a human and a *Sidhe* can never marry.'

'You said that you would marry me.'

'I cannot,' he said.

Dealba's face grew cold and angry. The air around her grew chill and frost formed on the leaves and branches. 'You will marry me,' the fairy woman warned.

Illan shivered with the cold. His fingers and toes grew numb and he saw streaks of white ice forming on his armour and glittering on the metal of his sword, which was still lying on the ground. He bent down to pick it up and when he straightened he shook his head. 'I will not marry you,' he said, 'I do not love you.'

Dealba pointed her hand at Illan and said something in the language of the *Sidhe*. Immediately, the air grew even colder and then the leaves on the bushes around the man froze one by one, until they were like glass. The branches hardened and turned to a silver colour and Illan's sword grew so cold that it burned his fingers and he had to drop it. When it hit the ground it broke apart. The fairy woman took a step backwards and began to fade into the night.

'Wait,' Illan said. He didn't want the banshee to put a curse on him — he would never be able to get rid of it. He reached out for the woman and his arm brushed against a branch. The leaves immediately shattered and fell apart with a tiny tinkling sound, like small silver bells. Illan stepped backwards with fright — and touched against another branch. It too shattered into a fine silvery dust, and as the man watched the whole clump of frozen bushes collapsed into dust all around him with the sound of breaking glass.

Finn and the rest of the guards came running up, their swords and spears ready.

'What happened?' Finn shouted. 'What was that noise?'

'A banshee,' Illan said quietly, beginning to grow warm now that the cold had vanished. He looked over at Finn. 'She has cursed me; what will I do?'

'What sort of curse?' Finn asked.

'I don't know — yet.'

The Captain of the Fianna looked troubled, and then he shook his head. 'There is nothing you can do but wait for the curse to catch up with you. When you know what it is you might be able to fight it.'

Illan and Tuirean were married a week later. The wedding was a huge happy affair, with all the Knights of the Fianna and the nobles and their ladies there. It started at sunrise when the chief priest, the Arch-Druid, married them in the first rays of the morning sun, and then it went on all day, eating, drinking and dancing, and later on there were contests and games. When night fell, the bards came and sat around the huge fires telling stories about the ancient peoples who had come to the land of Erin. They told about the woman called Caesir Banba who came from the land of Egypt and who had given her name to the island; they told about the terrible Fomorians, who were demons from the icy north, and they told about the magical Tuatha De Danann.

After the wedding, Tuirean and her husband headed off to Illan's palace in the north of the country where they would have a few days holiday before he had to return to his duties as one of the Fianna.

However, only two days later, a messenger arrived from Finn, asking Illan to come back immediately. He said that a huge pirate fleet had been sighted off the coast, and Finn wanted all his best men by his side if they did try to land.

Tuirean stood by the tall wooden gates of the fort and waved at her husband until he had rounded the bend in the road and was out of sight. She was turning to go back indoors when she heard the sound of hooves. She looked back, thinking that Illan might be returning for something he had forgotten. But it was not her husband, it was a young man, wearing a messenger's cloak. He pulled his horse to a stop a few feet away from Tuirean and climbed down. He bowed.

'My lady,' he said, 'has my lord Illan set off yet?'

Tuirean looked surprised. 'He left only a few minutes ago — but surely you passed him just around that bend?' she asked, pointing down the dusty road.

The young man smiled and shook his head. 'I'm sorry my lady, I saw no one.'

Tuirean shook her head in wonder. Even if Illan had been galloping, surely he wouldn't have reached the distant cross-roads so soon? 'Was there a message for my husband?' she asked then.

The messenger nodded again. He was a young man who looked no more than fifteen or sixteen, with a head of snow-white hair and sharp sort of face. 'I have a message for my lord Illan — and for you too, my lady,' he added with a smile.

'For me?'

'Yes, my lady. Finn fears that the pirates may land in some of the smaller bays around here and try and sneak south to attack him. He does not wish you to be caught out here with no one to protect you.'

'But the fort is guarded,' Tuirean said.

'I think Muiren, Finn's mother and your sister, has insisted that he bring you south for greater protection,' the messenger said.

Tuirean shook her long jet black hair and stamped her foot in annoyance. 'Sometimes my older sister is worse than a mother — always fussing.'

'But does that not show that she cares for you?' the messenger asked quietly.

But Tuirean said nothing and stamped off to pack a small satchel and have her horse saddled.

A little while later Tuirean and the messenger rode away from the fort and headed south in the same direction Illan had taken. They reached the crossroads by midday and then the messenger stopped. He leaned forward and pointed down one of the roads, 'That way.'

Tuirean hesitated. 'I thought it was this way,' she said, pointing down another road.

'We could go that way,' the messenger said, 'but this way is safer. It takes us away from the coast where the pirates might come ashore.'

Tuirean nodded doubtfully. She wasn't sure about that but she still followed the messenger down the side road. Soon they rode into a group of trees, short fat ancient oak trees with broad leaves and moss growing on the trunks. There was a little clearing beyond the trees and then the road continued on into a forest where the trees were growing so closely that their branches grew twisted together above the path and hid the sun and sky from their sight. Tuirean had to squint to see the path, and she could barely make out the shape of the messenger ahead of her.

Suddenly there was the sound of thunder overhead and then it began to rain. Hard heavy drops patted against the closely grouped leaves, spattering and splashing, but very few actually reached the ground below. The messenger raised his hand and stopped, but Tuirean was so close that her horse actually bumped into his.

'What's wrong?' she asked.

'Nothing,' the messenger said, 'but there is a clearing ahead and if we ride across it we will be soaked.'

Tuirean peered over his shoulder and saw what he meant. Ahead of them the trees had been cut away leaving an almost circular clearing through which the path ran in a straight line. She saw the rain then for the first time. It was falling straight down, drumming and thrumming onto the hard ground. Tuirean looked up into the sky, but all she saw were heavy full-looking grey clouds.

'How long will it last?' she asked the messenger.

He shrugged his shoulders. 'I don't know; not long, I hope.'

But the rain continued to pour down, soaking into the hard earth turning it to soft muck. Now water began to find its way down through the thick umbrella of leaves over their heads, and began to plink and drip onto the two riders, making them shiver and pull up their long riding cloaks.

'I think we should hurry on,' Tuirean said, pushing her long dark hair out of her eyes, 'we might be able to catch up with Illan.'

'Perhaps the lord Illan is also sheltering,' the messenger said.

Tuirean nodded. 'That's what I mean. If he is sheltering from this rain, we might just catch up with him.'

The messenger nodded slowly. 'Yes, we might,' he said, but he didn't move.

'Well, let's go then,' Tuirean said angrily.

'Stay where you are!'

Tuirean turned to look at the messenger in amazement. How dare he speak to her in that way! 'What did you say?' she demanded loudly.

'You heard me,' the messenger said rudely. He urged his horse forward, out into the centre of the clearing, and then he turned the animal around so that he was facing Tuirean again. The woman was about to speak again, when she noticed something strange about the messenger — all the colours in his clothes, his skin, his hair — even the colour of the horse — were being washed away, running like wet paint.

Tuirean closed her eyes, squeezed them hard and opened them again. But the colour was still running down the man in long streaks. It had started at his head: black streaks from his hair, mingled with the dark brown streaks from his skin and the brown from his eyes, ran down onto the front of his jerkin, and then the browns and greens of the cloth ran from that and dripped onto his legs. The

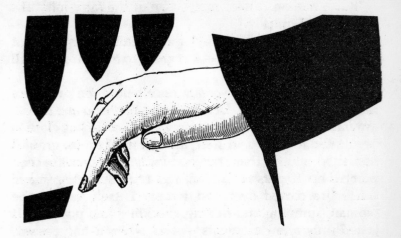

colours then fell onto the horse's back and soon its brown coat was dripping away into a dark mucky pool about its hooves.

Underneath he was white — snow white, ice white, cold white. And 'he' no longer looked like a 'he' — 'he' looked like a 'she'.

Tuirean looked at the creature and then felt her heart begin to pound with fright — it was a banshee! She tried to turn her horse around, but suddenly all the trees around her turned white with ice and frost. A tree cracked with the sudden weight of ice and sleet, and fell across her path, blocking the path. She turned back to the banshee.

'Who are you? What do you want?' she said as loud as she could.

The banshee smiled, showing her sharp white teeth. 'I am Dealba,' she said so softly that Tuirean had to strain to hear her, 'and I have come for you.'

Tuirean grew very frightened then. 'What do you mean?'

'You married Illan,' the banshee said.

'Yes,' Tuirean nodded, 'I married him.'

'But he should have married me,' Dealba suddenly shouted, 'he knew me first!'

'But a human cannot marry one of the fairy-folk,' the woman said quickly.

'He should have married me!' Dealba insisted. 'But since he will not have me — I'm going to make sure he will not have you either!'

Tuirean managed to scream once before the banshee's ice-magic touched her. Dealba raised her hand and the air around her froze so that the rain which was falling close to her turned to snow and sleet, and the mud on the ground hardened into ice that cracked loudly. The banshee then pointed her fingers at Tuirean, and a thin sparkling line of white fire darted over and wrapped itself around the woman, spinning and hissing, crackling and popping. It lasted only a few moments — and when it had passed, Tuirean had disappeared also, but in her place was a huge coal-black wolfhound. It glared at the banshee for a few moments, and then growled deep in its throat.

Dealba laughed quietly. 'If Illan will not have me,' she said to herself, 'then I will not allow him to have you.'

Now when Illan reached Finn's fort, he found that there were no pirates off Erin's coasts, and that Finn had not sent any messenger north for him. When he looked for the messenger who had brought him the message he could not be found. Illan grew frightened then, and thundered back to his fort, accompanied by Finn and some of the Knights of the Fianna. They knew something was amiss.

When they reached the fort, one of the guards there told Illan about the messenger who had come with the message from Finn for the lady Tuirean. And they had not seen her since then.

Illan raged and swore. He and the Fianna searched the surrounding countryside and he even hired men and sent them all over the country looking for his missing wife, but for a long time there was no sign of her.

Nearly a year passed.

It was high summer when Illan received a message from

Finn. The Lord of the Fianna had heard a strange story concerning Fergus, one of the western lords. Now this Fergus was well known for his dislike of dogs, because he had once been bitten on the leg when he was a boy and from that day would not allow a dog into his fort. But what was curious was that Fergus had been keeping a huge wolfhound for the past few months, and treating it very well indeed. And what was even stranger was that Fergus insisted that Finn had sent the dog to him for safe-keeping. But Finn insisted that he had sent no dog to this man and wanted Illan to investigate, so the knight saddled up his horse and set off on the long road to the west.

He had ridden a few miles down the road when something white flitted through the trees and stepped out onto the path. It was Dealba.

'What do you want?' Illan demanded.

The banshee smiled strangely. 'Where are you going?' she asked.

Illan was about to tell her but then stopped. 'Why do you want to know?' he asked.

Dealba smiled again. 'Perhaps you're heading into the west to visit Fergus, lord of the Seashore?'

Illan felt a strange chill run down his back. 'How do you know that?' he whispered.

The banshee smiled. 'I know many things,' she said.

'Do you know where my wife is then?' he asked.

'I might.'

'Where is she?' Illan suddenly shouted, making his horse jump and sending the birds in the trees up into the sky.

'She is with Fergus, lord of the Seashore,' Dealba said.

Illan knew then. 'And is she . . . is everything all right?' he asked.

'She is in good health,' Dealba said and then added with a grin, 'Fergus has been taking very good care of her.'

Illan suddenly pulled out his sword and pointed it at the fairy woman. 'You have changed her into a dog!' he shouted.

Dealba laughed. 'I have.'

'Change her back,' Illan said, 'or else . . .'

'Or else what?' Dealba asked. 'I could turn you into a block of ice before you had taken a single step close. But I will change her back into a human shape for you — for a price,' she added.

'And what is the price?' Illan asked with a sigh.

'You must come with me into the fairy fort.'

Illan didn't stop to think. 'Yes,' he said, 'I'll do it.'

Dealba disappeared in a rush of cold air, and then reappeared almost immediately with a huge black wolfhound by her side. As soon as the dog saw Illan it began to bark furiously and wag its tail back and forth.

'This is your wife,' the banshee said, and she touched the dog with the tips of her fingers. A white covering like snowflakes formed on the dog's hair. It grew thicker and thicker until the dog was buried beneath a mound of snow — and then it all suddenly fell away. And standing there in her human shape was Tuirean. She cried out with joy and ran over to her husband.

'You've saved me,' she said, 'I knew you would.'

Illan kissed her gently. 'But to save you I have to go with her,' he nodded towards Dealba, 'but don't worry, I will be back to you as soon as I can.'

'Must you go now?' Tuirean asked in a whisper, tears forming in her huge dark eyes.

'I must,' he said, 'but I will be back.'

Dealba reached out and touched Illan and he was immediately frozen within a block of ice. The banshee then touched the ice, and then both she and it disappeared in a glitter of silver snowflakes, leaving Tuirean standing alone.

A little more than a week later, Tuirean, who had been expecting a baby before she had been turned into the wolfhound, gave birth to twins. But they were not human twins — they were two lovely wolfhound cubs.

Tuirean gave the pups to Finn to care for. The greatest magicians and sorcerers in the land were called in to try and give the dogs a human appearance, but they couldn't, because the fairy magic was so strong.

And Finn named the pups Bran and Sceolan. They were magic hounds: faster, stronger and more intelligent than any other dog in the land of Erin. They were human hounds.

Finn's Dogs

In ancient times, it was quite common for kings of one country to send their sons to be educated and trained in another king's court. There were many reasons for this, but it also helped prevent wars. After all, a king would not be likely to attack another country if he knew his son was living there — would he?

There was even a time, when Arthur, son of the King of Britain, and a distant ancestor of the great King Arthur, was sent to Ireland to be trained as a warrior and a leader by the mighty Finn MacCumhal, leader of the Fianna. However, the young boy very nearly started a war between the two countries . . .

Finn MacCumhal stood on the hill top and looked down into the valley below. In the distance he could hear his men beating their shields and rattling their swords. They were making as much noise as possible to drive the savage wild boars before them into the valley where they would be trapped by the waiting hunters.

The tall warrior shaded his dark eyes and looked for his men. Luckily he couldn't see most of them — and that was the way it should be. His men were hidden in amongst the trees and bushes and if he could see them, then the boars, who would soon come snorting and stamping into the valley, might also spot them.

However, Finn could see something moving below. It was a flash of colour. The dark warrior frowned; he had told his men to dress only in greens and browns, and not to wear bright colours today. He had seen the movement from the far side of the valley, where some of the young men he was training were hidden. Someone had disobeyed him. He pointed with one short stubby finger. 'Who's over there?' he asked, without turning around.

A man stepped up behind him and looked over his shoulder. He was Oisin, Finn's son, and was deeply tanned and as dark-haired as his father. 'Ah, that would be the young British prince, Arthur,' he said. 'I put him over there to keep him out of harm's way.'

'He's wearing something coloured,' Finn said quietly, although his son recognised the anger in his voice.

'Is it red?' Oisin asked, and then continued as Finn nodded, 'I told him to leave that cloak behind him.'

The tall warrior shook his head. 'That boy is more trouble that he's worth. I've a good mind to send him back to his father.'

'That might not be wise,' Oisin said quietly. 'At least while he's here, his father will not launch an attack on us, and, because the merchants know that there will be no trouble, trade had increased.'

'He could be a spy, sent here to find out our strengths and numbers.'

Oisin shook his head and smiled. 'I doubt it; he's too stupid.'

Finn nodded. 'Aye, I suppose he is. I've also noticed he's a greedy young man.' He stopped then as a dozen and more large sharp-haired pigs smashed their way through the bushes below. 'Ah! Here come the boars . . .'

Arthur looked up when he heard the sudden crashing ahead of him. He gripped his long hunting spear tightly in both hands — and prayed that the savage animals would not come in his direction. Prince Arthur was almost twelve. He was a tall, thin boy with straw-coloured hair and very pale grey eyes. His face was thin and sharp, and his eyes were always moving, darting to and fro, and he never looked anyone in the face.

And, although there were princes and young lords from all over Erin, and from Britain, Scotland, the kingdom of Wales, and even from the lands further east, no one liked Arthur. He was a sly, secretive boy, who told lies and carried tales.

The crashing noise grew louder — and suddenly a huge boar broke through the bushes and stopped a short distance away from the boy. It snorted, its small black eyes as hard and as sharp as its two yellowed tusks. Arthur backed away slowly, holding the spear out in front of him. He tried to remember what Finn had taught him about boar-hunting and about how to hold a boar-spear, but the sight of the huge animal with its bristling short hair drove everything from his mind.

The animal lowered its head . . . it was going to charge.

Suddenly the bushes all around the terrified boy were torn asunder as three huge hunting dog came crashing through them. They stopped and gathered around the boy, and for a single moment, Arthur thought they were going to attack him. Then he realised that they were facing the boar, standing between it and him.

'They must be Finn's war-hounds,' he said to himself, looking at the huge dogs, each one of which was easily the size of a small horse.

The three dogs began growling then, and Arthur saw their backs stiffen. With savage growls they leaped at the boar. It squealed once and twisted away through the bushes, with the dogs snapping close behind.

Arthur gave a sigh of relief, and then stiffened as he heard more sounds close by. A clump of bushes on his right parted and a man stepped into the clearing. Arthur recognised Ector, one of his father's warriors who had come to Erin with him.

'Are you hurt?' the warrior demanded, looking quickly over the boy, but, except for his pale colour, he looked

unharmed. 'I saw the boars come this way . . .' he began.

'I'm fine,' Arthur said, 'I think I frightened him off.'

Ector nodded, relieved. If anything happened to the prince, he, and the eight other men who had been sent to act as his servants and guards, would be held responsible. His father's instructions to them before they had sailed for Erin had been simple, 'Watch over him, take care of him, and do whatever he wants.'

'I thought I heard Finn's war-hounds coming this way,' Ector said, looking around.

'Ah yes, they raced through here just before you arrived,' Arthur said. 'Tell me,' he asked then, 'just what's so special about those dogs?'

Ector leaned on his spear and ran the fingers of his right hand through his short grey beard. 'Well, you know that they're not supposed to be real dogs at all? Bran and Sceolan are actually related to Finn; his mother had been changed into a dog . . . or something.' The warrior shook his head. 'I'm not sure of the exact details. All I do know is that Bran, Sceolan and Adnuall are the finest hunting animals in all the known world.'

'Why hasn't my father bought them?' Arthur wondered.

'Because they're not for sale,' Ector said, 'your father, and indeed many other kings and princes, have offered Finn huge amounts of treasure, cattle, and land for the three dogs, but he refuses to part with them. You see,' he said, lowering his voice to a whisper, 'they are magical animals — and there are very few magical animals left in the world now.'

'I'm sure my father would like them,' Arthur said softly.

'I'm sure he would,' the warrior agreed, 'but Finn is hardly likely to give them to him, now is he?'

Arthur smiled craftily. 'Could we not just take them?' he said, very quietly.

Ector looked shocked. 'But that would be stealing . . .' he began.

'I'm sure my father would be very pleased if he got those animals as a present. He would be very pleased, wouldn't he?' he asked Ector.

'Well yes, but . . .'

'And I'm sure if I brought him those animals, he wouldn't be able to send me back here would he?'

'No, but . . .'

'So, if I bring him the dogs, I'll be able to stay at home, instead of here in this cold, wet country, where no one likes me.'

'Arthur, listen to me,' Ector said, 'if you steal those dogs from Finn, he will probably come after you for them, and more than likely declare war on Britain if he doesn't get them back.'

'Finn wouldn't dare! My father is the King of Britain.'

'Arthur,' Ector said gently, 'King's do not frighten Finn; nothing frightens Finn. I beg of you, do not even think about taking those dogs.'

But the prince shook his head stubbornly. 'No. I must have them.'

'I'm warning you not to!'

Arthur glared at the warrior. 'You have no right to warn me of anything; you have no right to tell me anything. I am Arthur, prince of Britain, soon to be king. I tell you what to do!'

Ector sighed. Arthur was one of the most difficult children he had ever met. He had a son of his own roughly around the same age, and the boy would never dare talk to any man that way. He could see why none of the other children liked the boy.

'I want those dogs, Ector, and I want them today. Now, listen to me. The hunt will be stopping shortly for something to eat. Everyone will be meeting down by the stream, and while the men are eating, I want you to find all my men and have them waiting in the woods with fresh horses. Then you and that foreign soldier, the blond-haired one who knows a little animal magic . . .'

'Olaf,' Ector whispered.

'Yes, that's the one. Find the three dogs, and have Olaf cast a spell on them.'

'What sort of spell?' Ector asked. 'You can't just make them fall asleep and carry them away. Have you seen the size of those dogs?'

'Well . . . well, have him cast a spell of obedience or something on them.'

'It might not work — they are magical creatures.'

'It better work,' Arthur said, smiling to himself, trying to imagine the look on his father's face when he gave him the three dogs.

A little while later, the short sharp blast of a hunting horn rang across the valley. It was the signal that the hunt was over for the moment and that some lunch was just about ready. One by one, and then in small groups, the men made their way out from the trees and bushes and down to the river bank.

Finn rode in with Oisin a little while later. He spoke briefly with some of the men, particularly with those who were new to the hunt, pointing out what they had done wrong, or indeed, how good they had been. At last he rode up to where Arthur was being served his meal by Ector, a little distance away from the rest of the men. The leader of the Fianna reined in his horse.

'I thought I gave instructions that no bright colours were to be worn today,' he said quietly, looking down at the boy who was still wearing his bright red cloak.

Arthur glanced up and then continued eating. 'I was cold,' he said at last.

'And very nearly dead too,' Finn said. 'If I hadn't sent Bran, Sceolan and Adnuall down to rescue you, you would have been torn to pieces by that boar.'

'I thought you said you frightened the boar off yourself,' Ector said, glaring at the boy.

'I did!' Arthur said sullenly.

'Do not lie to me, boy,' Finn snapped.

'They arrived too late,' Arthur snapped. 'I had driven the boar off by then. Anyway, how do you know what happened — you weren't even there.'

Finn smiled coldly. 'Why, Bran told me of course. We will not talk of this now, but you will come and see me in the morning . . . '

'I am prince of Britain,' Arthur interrupted, 'you can do nothing to me.'

'But you are not in Britain now,' Finn said, his voice growing very soft indeed, and all those who knew him knew that Finn only whispered when he was very angry. 'You are in Erin now, and you are in my care. I have a duty to your father to train you to be a warrior, and your father sent you to me because he respects me. In return I expect you to respect me, in other words, to honour me as you would your father.' Finn pulled on his horse's rein, and the animal daintily side-stepped. 'You will see me in the morning.' Finn then nodded to Ector and rode away, followed by Oisin.

Arthur glared after the two riders. 'You won't be seeing me tomorrow,' he whispered. 'Are my men ready?' he suddenly asked Ector.

The Knight nodded, without saying anything.

'Let's go then.'

Arthur and Ector made their way down along the river bank, following the sounds of barking and yapping. They stopped before a huge clump of thorn bushes and peered out across the clearing to where Faolan the Hound-Master was feeding the animals and checking their paws for any signs of splinters or thorns.

'Where's Olaf?' Arthur whispered in Ector's ear.

'Here!'

Both of them jumped with fright at the sound of the rough harsh voice behind them. They turned around to find the huge northerner crouching down beside a tree trunk, grinning widely. They had walked right by him without noticing. He stood up and made his way over to the bushes without making a sound. Olaf was huge, even taller than most of the Fianna. He had bright blue eyes and he wore his blond hair in two long plaits down his back. There was an enormous battle-axe slung over his shoulder.

'What do you want me to do?' he asked the boy in his strange accent.

'I want those three dogs,' Arthur said pointing to Bran, Sceolan and Adnuall, who were sitting a little apart from the rest of the dogs devouring a huge bone between them.

'Good dogs,' Olaf murmured, pulling at his beard. 'Good dogs,' he said again, 'the best I've seen. Why do you want them?'

'As a gift for my father,' Arthur said quickly. 'Now, what I want you to do is to cast some sort of spell over them, something that will make them follow you.'

The huge man shook his head. 'That might be difficult. There is a lot of magical blood in them — they might not follow me, and besides, even if we do get them, Finn and the Fianna will some after us. We wouldn't have a chance of escaping.'

'They won't follow us to Britain,' Arthur said.

'I wouldn't be too sure of that,' Ector said doubtfully. 'Finn would probably follow those dogs into the Otherworld.'

'We must hurry; the hunt will be starting soon,' Arthur said to Olaf. 'Now you Ector must distract the Hound-Master.'

'How?'

'I don't know. Talk to him or something.'

'And what do I do if he won't be distracted?' Ector asked.

'Well then knock him out. But hurry, hurry!'

While Ector crept back through the bushes so that he could walk up the path to Faolan, Olaf began casting his spell. First he took a small leather bag from around his neck and, after clearing a space on the ground, tipped everything in it onto the clearing. Arthur, who had been peering over his shoulder and had been expecting to see something marvellous, was disappointed to find that there seemed to be nothing more than a series of polished white sticks.

'These are the bones of all the hunting animals that walk in these lands,' Olaf said quietly. 'Everything from the largest wolf to the smallest rat is here.'

'What are those markings there?' Arthur asked pointing to the scratches on the bones.

'They are Runes. It is a form of writing something like your Ogham writing. But this is magical. Now watch. First we pick the bones for a dog, and I suppose I should use those for a wolf also,' he added, picking out two tiny bones and setting them to one side. 'Now we do this . . .'

There were voices from the other side of the bushes as Ector wandered up to Faolan. 'A fine hunt so far eh?'

'Yes, very fine.'

'Your animals are magnificent.'

'Ah yes; they are the finest in all the known world, I dare say.'

The Runes had now been set out and arranged in a certain way, so that they formed a rough star shape, pointing inwards to the wolf and dog bones which were crossed in the middle. As Arthur watched, Olaf spread his broad hands over the design, closed his eyes and began to mutter in his strange language. For a while nothing seemed to happen, and then the prince saw a strange reddish-black glow seeping out from between the northerner's fingers. Suddenly, Olaf opened his eyes and looked at Arthur — and the boy nearly screamed aloud, because Olaf's bright blue eyes had turned into two red-black coals.

The huge warrior stood up and, raising his right hand, he pointed towards the three dogs with his first and little fingers.

But the sudden sound made Faolan turn around. He stopped in amazement at the sight of the huge man with the burning eyes pointing at his three prize dogs, and then he reached for his sword. 'You . . !' he began, and stopped when the northerner's head turned slowly and looked at the Hound-Master.

'Get away from those dogs,' Faolan shouted and he began to charge at him with his raised sword.

Olaf pointed his finger at the Hound-Master, and a thin red-black spark hopped from its tip to the point of Faolan's sword. The sword was suddenly snatched from the man's hand and spun through the air, and then it embedded itself in the soft earth, where it began to melt into a pool of molten metal.

Faolan looked at the bubbling pool on the ground for a horrified moment and then he scrambled for his hunting horn. He had raised it to his lips when Ector struck him from behind, knocking him unconscious.

However, all the dogs had been disturbed by the magic, and began to bark and howl. Suddenly Bran, Sceolan and Adnuall leaped up and charged toward the northerner, howling like demons, their long yellow fangs bared.

Olaf pointed at the nearest dog, Sceolan, and once more a thin red-black spark hopped from his finger towards the animal. It seemed to buzz around the dog for a few heartbeats and then it jumped onto his coat and disappeared. Suddenly the dog's long haired coat seemed to take on a life of its own, and stood straight out from his body — and then the dog stopped still, frozen in place.

The second animal, Adnuall, having seen what had just happened, dived into the bushes, and Olaf's red-black spark missed the dog by a fraction and fastened onto a bush. The bush hummed softly, as if a swarm of bees were trapped inside, and then it slowly turned into a pile of fine grey ash.

But Olaf's second try didn't miss and, like Sceolan, Adnuall froze into position with the hair on his coat standing on end.

Now only Bran remained. But Bran was the smartest of the three dogs. The northerner's first spark missed him, and turned another bush to ash, and his second spark struck a tree. Arthur and Ector watched fascinated as the bark of the tree quickly turned grey, and then this grey mould raced up along the branches and out into the leaves, and then, with a soft whispering sound, the tree crumbled to dust.

Bran knew that he couldn't hope to escape for long if he remained hidden amongst the trees and bushes, but there was the river. If he could get into the water, Olaf's magic might not work then; Bran knew that a lot of magic wouldn't work on water.

The dog raced through the woods towards the river bank, while behind him, bush after bush, and tree after tree turned to piles of grey dust. But there was water ahead of him now, he could see it gleaming blue and sparkling through the trees . . .

Bran dived into the water . . . just as the northerner's spark touched him. And then it seemed as if the whole river had gone mad. The water began to bubble and boil, and fish of all shapes and sizes jumped wriggling up into the air, and flopped onto the river bank, frozen into position.

But Bran too had been caught by the magic, and was now stuck half-in and half-out of the water, with only the back half of his body showing, his head under water.

'Quick, quick, before he drowns,' Arthur shouted at Olaf.

The warrior slowly shook his head and the red-black glow died from his eyes, returning them to blue. However, now the northerner looked pale and tired, as if the magic had drained him. 'Come Bran, come,' he said wearily, 'come to me.'

For a moment nothing happened, and Arthur was just beginning to think that Olaf's magic had failed, when the dog's legs quivered, and it slowly heaved itself out of the water, turned around and came trotting slowly over to them.

'Come Sceolan, come Adnuall,' Olaf called, and the two dogs also trotted over to him. 'Sit,' he commanded, and they sat. Olaf looked down at the prince. 'We have them,' he said.

Arthur looked at the dogs and smiled. They looked exactly the same as they had before — only now their eyes were a deep red-black. 'We have them,' he said. 'Come on, we better go before Finn and his Knights get here.'

'There's been magic worked here,' Finn said, a few moments later when he and Oisin with the rest of the Fianna came running into the clearing. 'I can taste the magic on the air.'

'But what happened?' his son asked, looking around at the great piles of grey dust.

Finn sucked his thumb as he looked around, and as he did so, his eyes became distant, as if he were looking at something only he saw. At last he took his thumb out of his mouth, and said, so softly that only Oisin, who was standing beside him, heard. 'Magic. I see magic — animal magic, fire-magic, powerful magic, taming-magic . . .'

'Taming-magic?' Oisin asked quietly, 'What is taming magic?'

His father shook his head. 'Old magic . . . old magic . . . red magic . . . northern magic . . . animal magic. Animals!' He suddenly shouted, turning to Oisin. 'Count the dogs! Where are Bran, Sceolan and Adnuall?'

Oisin looked around in surprise. He knew he had missed something; it was the familiar three huge dogs.

One of the Knights of the Fianna brought Faolan to Finn. The Hound-Master was holding his head, and looked pale and sick.

'What happened?' Finn asked gently.

'I'm not sure,' Faolan said, shaking his head, and then wishing he hadn't. 'First, there was a man — a stranger by his voice — and he seemed eager to talk. And then . . . and then . . . and then there was another man,' the Hound-Master said slowly, 'but bigger this time, a giant of a man, with long blond hair, and a pale beard — and red eyes.'

'Red eyes?' Oisin asked.

'Yes, red eyes, eyes of fire. He pointed a finger at me, and my sword flew from my hand and . . . and melted into the ground. And then . . . and then I don't know. Someone hit me; the first man I think. I can't remember. I'm sorry, my lord; it's my fault the three best hounds in Erin have been lost.'

'No, it's not your fault,' Finn said quickly. 'I'm sure you did the best you could. Besides, there was little you could do against magic.'

'But who could have taken them?' Faolan asked. 'Who would be so stupid.'

'Oh, I have a very good idea,' the leader of the Fianna said in a whisper. 'Come, Oisin, we have work to do,' he said, walking away.

Oisin followed his father down to the river bank. When they were away from the clearing with its howling dogs and shouting men, Finn sat down on a tree stump and stared out across the water. His son sat down by his feet.

'Well, who do you think . . . ?' Finn asked.

'Well, the man with the strange accent might be Ector, and the huge man with the blond hair and beard can only be Olaf — although Olaf has bright blue eyes.'

'But animal-magic is sometimes called red-magic,' his father said quietly.

'Would it give the magician red-eyes?'

Finn nodded without saying a word.

'Both Ector and Olaf are Prince Arthur's men,' Oisin said softly.

Finn nodded again. 'I know.'

'But why would he even attempt to steal the dogs?' Oisin asked in amazement. 'Surely he knows he can't get far?'

Finn sucked his thumb for a few moments, calling up the magic of the Salmon of Knowledge. 'Arthur thinks that if he gives the three dogs as a present to his father, then the king will bring him home from Erin.'

'And will he?'

'Of course not. If Arthur gives him the dogs, the king will just send them right back to me. He doesn't want a war with the Fianna Erin.'

'But will the boy give the dogs to his father?' Oisin asked then.

Finn smiled and nodded. 'Ah, that is a good question. Arthur is greedy, and that greed might trap him. He knows there is nothing like Bran, Sceolan and Adnuall in the whole world. It is my guess that once he reaches Britain's shores, he will probably hunt with the animals just to test them. Once he does that and sees how powerful they are and, more importantly, how powerful they make him, he won't give them up. You know Oisin,' Finn said, looking at his son, 'with those three dogs alone, you could defeat an army.'

'We have to get them back.'

'I know,' the leader of the Fianna said wearily.

'Where are they now?' Oisin asked.

Finn sucked his thumb again. 'They are on board a small craft skimming across the waves towards Britain's shores. Arthur is there, with all his men — and the three dogs.'

'It must be a magical craft then if its moving so fast with all that weight,' Oisin said.

'No . . . no, strangely enough, it's not a magical craft. Ah,' he said then, 'the northerner has called up a magical breeze to push them along.'

'Well then, I'll go after them,' Oisin said quickly, jumping to his feet. 'Can you call up a wind for me and my men?'

'Better than that, I can call up a wind and Ferdoman the Half-*Sidhe* can call up a magical wave. One will push you along, and the second will carry you. They might land in Britain before you, but you will not be far behind.'

'Right,' Oisin said, 'I'll get my brothers, Raighen and Fainche.'

'Bring Faolan,' Finn said. 'He is the only one the dogs will go to, and I suppose you should bring Goll also, just in case you have to fight that northern giant.'

'We'll bring Bran, Sceolan and Adnuall back, father.'

Finn looked at his son and nodded.

Soon a small wood-and-leather craft was skimming its way across the waves, its broad, square sail bulging before a stiff breeze. Oisin sat in the front of the craft, while Raighen, Fainche and Faolan sat in the middle of the boat. Goll — whose nickname was Mountain, because of his huge size — sat at the back of the craft, and he was so heavy that Oisin's end of the boat was actually up out of the water.

'Can you see anything yet?' Goll rumbled.

'Nothing but the sea,' Oisin said.

'Are you sure we're going in the right direction?' Goll asked.

'No!'

Goll sat up straight and very nearly capsized the craft. 'What . . .?' he began.

'We're going in the direction my father told the wind and the waves to take us. I'm sure it's the right direction. Now, stop worrying, we'll get there.'

'Well, I hope so,' Goll grumbled, 'I don't like the water; it's always wet and cold and it gets in my ears and up my nose.'

'Oh, don't be such a moan,' Faolan snapped. He had a terrible headache, and he was in no mood for Goll's moans and groans. The huge man always had something to grumble about, and yet he was one of the kindest of the Fianna, and also one of its bravest warriors.

'I see something,' Oisin said suddenly. 'Something grey, like a cloud, but it's not cloud.'

'Land,' Goll said, with a satisfied smile.

Almost as if the boat sensed land, it seemed to pick up speed and soon it was almost flying over the choppy waves in towards the rocky shore.

'I hope this knows how to stop!' Goll said with a squeak of alarm as they approached the beach much too fast.

Suddenly the boat stopped. It didn't hit anything, it just stopped dead. Oisin, who had been leaning out over the edge, was thrown headfirst into the water, while Raighen and Fainche, his two brothers, were also tossed over the side. Goll, who had been holding tightly onto the sides of the craft, was also thrown overboard — still clutching two handfuls of crushed wood. Only Faolan remained in the boat, and he was tossed about, knocking his head again. He sat up, holding his head in both hands, and looked around. He was dizzy and had a terrible pain in his head. 'I wish I hadn't come,' he said, with a groan.

A few miles inland, Arthur, his nine Knights and the three dogs were resting at the foot of a low rounded hill. Olaf's magical breeze had run out just as they sighted the shore, and the warriors had had to row their way inland, using their flat shields as oars. Once they had reached the beach, they had hurried away inland, knowing that either Finn or some of the Fianna would be close behind. However, they had to carry Olaf, who was exhausted from calling up the magical wind so soon after his animal magic, and this slowed them down. But, even though the northern sorcerer was exhausted, his spell continued to hold, and the three dogs were still under his control.

As they sat in the shade of an ancient oak tree, Arthur turned to Ector, who was sitting beside him, leaning back against the rough bark of the tree. 'Are you sure Finn will send someone after us?'

Ector nodded tiredly. 'Without a doubt. I wouldn't be surprised to see them come marching over that hill right now.'

'But we are in Britain,' Arthur protested.

'You do have Finn's dogs,' Ector reminded him, 'and nothing means more to Finn than his dogs. I don't think he would get as upset if his son was kidnapped. Our only hope now is to get to your father's court as quickly as possible, and pray that he can protect us from Finn's rage.'

'Too late,' Olaf murmured, 'too late.' The huge man was still half asleep, and seemed to be dreaming.

Ector suddenly stood up, and pulled out his sword. 'It is too late!' He pointed with his sword.

The eight Knights saw Oisin, with his brothers Raighen and Fainche, followed by Goll and Faolan, come charging down the hill towards them, their swords and spears ready.

'There's only five of them,' Arthur said with a grin, 'and there's nine of us — well, eight awake,' he said, looking at Olaf. 'Nine if you count me. We should be a match for them.'

'Ah, but they are Fianna,' Ector said sadly, 'and no one is a match for the Fianna. We are all dead men.'

The battle was short and furious and Arthur's Knights fought well, but they were no match for the Fianna, who were the finest warriors in the known world. Even huge Olaf — who had been awakened by the noise — was defeated by Goll, and as soon as this happened the red-black light died in the three dog's eyes. And then they too joined in the fight.

Soon only Arthur remained standing. But when Faolan was about to stab him with his spear, Goll stepped in front of him, and raised a hand.

'You cannot kill him; not yet anyway.'

'Why not?' Faolan demanded. 'His men knocked me out and stole my animals — and ruined one of my best swords also. I'm going to kill him.'

'But he is not yours to kill,' Goll said. 'He stole Finn's animals, and don't forget, Finn is also your commander.'

Faolan looked so disappointed that Goll had to laugh. 'But don't worry, I'm sure if Finn decides to kill him, he'll let you do it!'

Oisin knelt on the ground and the three dogs crowded in around him, barking happily and wagging their tails furiously. 'Come on,' he said, 'let's go home.'

However, Finn didn't kill Arthur. When he was taken back to Erin, he was made to swear a great oath to be one of Finn's followers for the rest of his days, and to pay him a tribute every year.

Some people were surprised because Arthur got away so lightly, but if the truth were only known, Finn didn't really care what happened to the boy as long as he got his dogs back and, by sparing his life, Finn had gained the undying friendship of the King of the Britons. During his lifetime there was never war between the two countries.

GREEN & GOLDEN TALES SERIES

IRISH FAIRY TALES
Michael Scott

'He found he was staring directly at a leprechaun. The small man was sitting on a little mound of earth beneath the shade of a weeping willow tree... The young man could feel his heart beginning to pound. He had seen leprechauns a few times before but only from a distance. They were very hard to catch, but if you managed at all to get hold of one...'

Michael Scott's exciting stories capture all the magic and mystery of Irish folklore. This collection of twelve fairy tales, beautifully and unusually illustrated, include:

The arrival of the Tuatha de Danann in Erin

The fairy horses	The King's secret
The crow goddess	The fairies' revenge
The wise woman's payment	The shoemaker and himself
The floating island	The sunken town

IRISH ANIMAL TALES
Michael Scott

'Have you ever noticed how cats and dogs sometimes sit up and look at something that is not there? Have you ever seen a dog barking at nothing? And have you ever wondered why? Perhaps it is because the animals can see the fairy folk coming and going all the time, while humans can only see the Little People at certain times...'

This illustrated collection of Michael Scott's strange stories reveal a wealth of magical creatures that inhabit Ireland's enchanted animal kingdom. The tales tell of the king of the cats, the magical cows, the fox and the hedgehog, the dog and the leprechaun, March, April and the Brindled Cow, the cricket's tale... A collection to entrance readers, both young and old.

THE CHILDREN'S BOOK OF IRISH FAIRY TALES
Patricia Dunn

The five exciting stories in this book tell of the mythical, enchanted origins of Irish landmarks when the countryside was peopled with good fairies, wicked witches, gallant heroes and beautiful princesses.

Did you know that there are bright, shimmering lakes in Killarney concealing submerged castles, mountain peaks in Wexford created by magic, a dancing bush in Cork bearing life-saving berries, the remains of a witch in a Kerry field and deer with silver and golden horns around Lough Gartan and Donegal?

These stories tell of extraordinary happenings long, long ago and show that evidence of these exciting events can still be seen today if you only take the time to look carefully.

ENCHANTED IRISH TALES
Patricia Lynch

Enchanted Irish Tales tells of ancient heroes and heroines, fantastic deeds of bravery, magical kingdoms, weird and wonderful animals... This new illustrated edition of classical folktales, retold by Patricia Lynch with all the imagination and warmth for which she is renowned, rekindles the age-old legends of Ireland, as exciting today as they were when first told. The collection includes:
- Conary Mór and the Three Red Riders
- The Long Life of Tuan Mac Carrell
- Finn Mac Cool and the Fianna
- Oisin and The Land of Youth
- The Kingdom of The Dwarfs
- The Dragon Ring of Connla
- Mac Datho's Boar
- Ethne